Blessed Are the Peacemakers

Biblical Perspectives on Peace and Its Social Foundations

...

edited by
Anthony J. Tambasco

PAULIST PRESS   New York / Mahwah

ACKNOWLEDGEMENTS

Selections from St. Augustine, *The City of God* in *A Select Library of the Nicene and Post-Nicene Fathers of the Christian Church* vol. 2, edited by Philip Schaff. Reprinted in 1979 by Wm. B. Eerdmans, Grand Rapids, Michigan. Permission granted by Wm. B. Eerdmans. Selections from *Luther's Works* vol. 46: *The Christian in Society,* edited by Robert C. Schultz. Copyright © 1967 by Fortress Press, Philadelphia, Pennsylvania. Permission granted by the publisher.

This book has been published with the generous support of the Catholic Biblical Association of America and its executive board. The opinions of the authors do not necessarily reflect the official position of the Catholic Biblical Association.

Book design by Ellen Whitney

Library of Congress Cataloging-in-Publication Data

Blessed are the peacemakers : biblical perspectives on peace and its
    social foundations / [compiled] by Anthony J. Tambasco.
        p.   cm.
    Papers from a task force organized at the annual meetings of the
Catholic Biblical Association between 1982 and 1986.
    Includes bibliographies and index.
    Contents: Introduction : Method and content of peace studies /
Anthony J. Tambasco—War and peace : a methodological
consideration / James A. Fischer—Wisdom literature, women's
culture, and peace / Kathleen M. O'Connor—Matthew 5:9 : "Blessed
are the peacemakers, for they shall be called sons of God" / Hugh M.
Humphrey—Peace and praise in Luke / David P. Reid—
Principalities, powers, and peace / Anthony J. Tambasco—The early
Christian tradition on peace and conflict resolution / Robert J.
Daly—Inspired authors and saintly interpreters in conflict : the
New Testament on war and peace / David Whitten Smith.
    ISBN 0-8091-3027-0 (pbk.) : $8.95 (est.)
    1. Peace—Biblical teaching.   2. Bible—Criticism, interpretation,
etc.   3. Peace—Religious aspects—Catholic Church.   4. Catholic
Church—Doctrines.   I. Tambasco, Anthony J.
BS680.P4B57   1989
261.8'73—dc19   88-29977
                                                                          CIP

Published by Paulist Press
997 Macarthur Boulevard
Mahwah, NJ 07430

Printed and bound in the
United States of America

CONTENTS

. .

iii

AUTHORS

. .

ROBERT J. DALY, S.J. Professor of theology and director of the Jesuit Institute at Boston College, with works such as *Christian Sacrifice* (1978), *Christian Biblical Ethics* (1984) and *Christians and the Military* (1985), has consistently studied the biblical and patristic foundations of Christian theology and life.

JAMES A. FISCHER, C.M., S.T.L., S.S.L. Seminary professor of Sacred Scripture, 1943–88 at various seminaries. Provincial of Vincentian Fathers, 1962–71; past-President of Catholic Biblical Association, 1978. Author of *The Psalms, God Created Woman, How to Read the Bible, Priests:* co-author of *Christian Biblical Ethics*.

HUGH M. HUMPHREY. Associate professor of religious studies at Fairfield University, Fairfield, Connecticut. He is the author of *A Bibliography for the Gospel of Mark: 1954–1980* (New York and Toronto: Edwin Mellen Press, 1981) and is a reviewer of books for the *Biblical Theology Bulletin*.

KATHLEEN M. O'CONNOR. Associate professor of biblical studies at the Maryknoll School of Theology, Maryknoll, New York. She has also served on the faculty of Providence College, Providence, Rhode Island, and is the author of *The Wisdom Literature*, Message of Biblical Spirituality 5 (Wilmington: Michael Glazier, 1988). She holds a Ph.D. in biblical studies from Princeton Theological Seminary.

DAVID P. REID, SS.CC. Studied in Rome (S.S.L., S.T.D.). After eighteen years at the Washington Theological Union, he is currently developing his pastoral aspirations in inner-city parish work in Rochester, New York. His concern is to relate Bible and life and this concern leads him to write on family and peace.

DAVID WHITTEN SMITH. Associate professor of theology (New Testament) and director of the justice and peace studies pro-

gram at the College of Saint Thomas, Saint Paul, Minnesota. He
holds an S.T.D. from the Angelicum University, Rome, and an
S.S.L. from the Pontifical Biblical Commission after studies at the
Catholic University, Washington, D.C. and the Ecole Biblique, Jerusalem. He has served as president of the Upper Midwest Region
of the Society of Biblical Literature.

ANTHONY J. TAMBASCO.   Associate professor of theology at
Georgetown University. He has an S.S.L. in Scripture, and a Ph.D.
in Christian ethics from Union Theological Seminary of New York.
Among his writings are three books, *The Bible for Ethics*, *In the Days
of Jesus*, and *What Are They Saying About Mary?* as well as articles in
other books and in periodicals, dealing with the use of the Bible for
ethics.

PREFACE

. .

This book derives from a "task force" (a seminar with several years' continuance) organized at the annual meetings of the Catholic Biblical Association (CBA) by a group of its members. This task force grew out of two prior projects. In 1983, the U.S. Catholic Bishops' Conference issued a pastoral letter which had been germinating for several years, *The Challenge of Peace*, with a call to further dialogue and discussion of this vital topic of our times. Critique of the preparatory drafts, as well as of the final document, indicated that the biblical section was not clearly related to what followed; more work was needed on the biblical background. In addition there was need to discuss how to implement the principles of the document. The challenges from this project prompted Rev. David Reid of the Washington Theological Union in Silver Spring, Maryland, and Dr. Anthony Tambasco of Georgetown University in Washington, D.C., to begin a seminar to discuss the social foundations of peace especially from a biblical perspective.

At the same time, a second project was nearing completion. A previous task force of the CBA was publishing a book dealing with hermeneutics (or the question of method in biblical interpretation), specifically with the issue of how to relate the Bible to Christian ethics. The book appeared in 1984 under the title, *Christian Biblical Ethics. From Biblical Revelation to Contemporary Christian Praxis: Method and Content*. Several members of that task force wanted to continue study of that issue by moving from the general discussion to a specific area of ethics. The challenge of relating the Bible to the specific ethical issue of peace provided that opportunity.

Thus was born in 1982 a seminar which would become in subsequent years a task force and which would meet at each annual convention until 1986, with a twofold study purpose:

the hermeneutical discussion of how to relate the Bible to Christian ethics, and the exegetical discussion of what the Bible might say about war and peace in our nuclear age. Six members of the earlier task force chose to participate in this new project. Besides Dr. Anthony Tambasco, they were Rev. Robert Daly, S.J. of Boston College; Rev. James Fischer, C.M. of St. Thomas Theological Seminary, Denver; Rev. Lawrence Frizzell of Seton Hall University, South Orange, NJ; Rev. Justin Pierce, S.D.S. of Silver Lake College, Manitowoc, WI; and Dr. Stanley Polan of Franklin Pierce College, Rindge, NH. In addition, the following who had not been part of the earlier study joined the new task force along with Rev. David Reid: Dr. Hugh Humphrey of Fairfield University in Connecticut, Dr. Kathleen O'Connor of Maryknoll School of Theology in New York, Most Rev. Richard Sklba, Auxiliary Bishop of Milwaukee, and Rev. David Smith of the College of St. Thomas in St. Paul, MN. While not all of these members submitted articles which would find their way to this book, all actively contributed to discussion of the studies that were written and thereby contributed indirectly to this final product.

Acknowledgement should be given to Dr. George Martin, an associate member of the CBA, who participated in almost all of the meetings, and also to other active and associate CBA members who shared in discussions in one or another of the annual meetings: Sr. Barbara Bozak, C.S.J.; Rev. Pedro Corbellini, C.S.; Rev. Edward Crowley; Sr. Dorothy Dawes, O.P.; Sr. Mary Ann Getty, R.S.M.; Dr. Alan Jenks; Dr. Everett Kalin; Rev. Raphael O'Loughlin, C.S.B.; Sr. Rosalie Ryan, C.S.J.; Dr. John Schmitt; Rev. Carroll Stuhlmueller, C.P.; Rev. Emil Wcela; and Mr. James Zeigler. Finally, the authors of this volume wish to thank the Catholic Biblical Association for its substantial subsidy and its encouragement. While the following work is not speaking for the association as such, and is the responsibility only of the authors, their work would not have been possible without the context provided by the Association at its annual meetings.

METHOD AND CONTENT OF PEACE STUDIES

. . . . . .

Anthony J. Tambasco

Two issues are of intense interest in Christian ethics to-day: world peace and the issue of the relationship of the Bible to contemporary Christian ethics. The following chapters deal with these two topics from the standpoint of biblical scholarship. The first issue is an exegetical concern, i.e., with deriving content or teaching on peace from the Bible. A biblical scholar's most direct contribution to world peace is this exegetical work. The following pages will suggest teaching from the Bible on the meaning of peace and even more especially on the social foundations for the work of peace. However, in order to derive content from the Bible, one must be conscious of methodology. Different methods can give radically different convictions about what the Bible is teaching, and to a great extent the content one will "find" is determined in advance by the method one chooses to use. For that reason, the concern for a proper or appropriate method for interpretation is prior to the actual work of interpretation. In technical language, Bible scholars say that hermeneutics (method of interpretation) is prior to exegesis (the actual work of interpretation; deriving the biblical teaching). The following studies give conscious advertence to the methods of using the Bible for teaching on peace.

Since hermeneutics is so important in this study, it might be helpful to introduce and discuss it in this opening section. The work of the following chapters builds on the hermeneutical study in *Christian Biblical Ethics. From Biblical Revelation*

Contemporary Christian Praxis: Method and Content.[1] The wide discussion on general principles of hermeneutics in that earlier book now becomes a narrower discussion of how these principles apply specifically to using the Bible for teaching on peace. In the following paragraphs we will highlight the content of *Christian Biblical Ethics* and indicate how its hermeneutical methods are further developed and illustrated in this book dealing with peace in the Bible.

Need for Hermeneutical Considerations

The previous task force of the Catholic Biblical Association was concerned to take some initial steps to bridge the gap between biblical scholarship and ethical studies. Biblical exegesis focuses on "what the text meant," i.e., on the intention of the author of the biblical text within that author's own history, sources, cultural influences, and community needs, etc. Even when one studies the ethical content of the Bible and attempts to systematize this content, the results can remain confined to the historical limits of the biblical era. We end up with the "Ethics of Paul" or the "Ethics of Jesus" as a survey of "what the text *meant*" in that history. Exegetes often abdicate responsibility and pass on to ethicists the task of determining "what the text *means*," i.e., the contemporary application of biblical teaching.

On the other hand, ethicists have generally been less than successful in their biblical considerations, as Birch and Rasmussen have pointed out.[2] Fundamentalism claims to apply the Bible directly and immediately to moral norms, but in doing so does not respect the historical conditionedness of the biblical text and the difference between the biblical and the contemporary context. Protestant Neo-Orthodoxy claims that human reasoning cannot be trusted and relies on biblical material to obtain moral norms independently of human reason. However, this approach recognizes neither the role that human reasoning has played in the systematizing of biblical ethics nor the continuing process of God's revelation in the world and in history. Often older Roman Catholicism and Liberal Protestantism began with preconceived notions of human nature and presupposed ethical systems, and then chose biblical proof-texts as support. In attempting to correct this tendency to proof-texting, more recent ethicists often use the Bible as general introduction for Christian life or as motivating force, but without any real effort to bring it into play on specific contemporary moral issues.

Christian Biblical Ethics builds from the observation that if ethics and, in fact, all theology is truly to be Christian, then it must center on the risen Christ as a living presence. Since, however, the experience of Christ's presence grows, among other things, out of biblical revelation, then somehow the Bible must be integral to the entire process of doing theology and ethics. We must have truly Christian *biblical* ethics. If such is the case, then the question arises of whether one adequately uses the biblical text if one takes it simply to provide the starting point for ethics, but does not involve it in the entire ethical process itself. The position of the CBA task force was that this was not an adequate position and that theologians needed to integrate the Bible more fully in the entire process of doing ethics, from theory to specific cases to actions.

To use the Bible in this more integrated way is not to imply that human reason or human experience is to be superseded or disqualified. In fact a full definition of biblical revelation needs to include present human experience as part of the context which enables us to derive meaning adequately from the biblical text. Thus, the task force offered this definition:

> Christian biblical revelation is the written record and faith-recollection of particular entrances of the divine into the realm of the human as recorded by the Jewish and Christian faith communities which experienced them and continue to live by them. Thus, Christian biblical revelation

> is that written history and recollected experience not only
> as it has been recorded in the Bible, but also as it is *now*
> being appropriated (continuing revelation) in the human
> and religious experience, knowledge and understanding
> of those living in a Christian faith community, i.e., in peo-
> ple attempting to live according to the reality and conse-
> quences of the divine entrances into the realm of the
> human.[3]

Thus, on this definition of biblical revelation we include not
only the written word as a source from the past, but the Scriptures as actualized through tradition and as lived in the present
with a view toward the future. Human reason and human experience are part of the process which interprets and gives
meaning to the biblical word.

A crucial observation thus follows for an adequate method
of relating the Bible to ethics: biblical revelation as we have
defined it evolves in a hermeneutical circle, i.e., there is a cir-
cular methodology involved in interpreting the Bible. The Bible produces faith-life, gives rise to faith-filled community and
explains human experience. However, faith-life produced the
written Bible; the texts came out of particular faith-filled human experiences which influenced the very act of writing.
Moreover, faith-life influences the interpretation of the biblical text today; Christians approach the Bible from the perspectives of their present faith as lived in their personal and
communal human experiences in the contemporary world.

David Kelsey has offered a helpful analysis of this hermeneutical circle.[4] He says that interpretation of the Bible depends on prior imaginative judgments, i.e., on presupposed
individual and communal self-images and on related images of
how God is experienced as present. The meaning sought from
the Bible depends on how it is used, and its use is shaped by
how God is pictured within the community. The exegete and
the ethicist are concerned not so much with answering the
question "What does the Bible say?" as with answering the
question "What is God using the Bible to do?" The answers

depend on the presuppositions we have about God's mode of presence and power. These presuppositions are derived in large part from our own historical context, from our human experience in the world as that is suffused also by present faith experience. More than anything else, Kelsey has made us conscious of the important role that presupposed world views play in our use and interpretation of the Bible. The CBA task force built on that point in *Christian Biblical Ethics*, and extended it to consider not only the presuppositions of the biblical interpreter, but those of the biblical author as well.

In the end, biblical theology tends to be an imagination-dominated interpretation of what was predominantly a product of the imagination in the first place. This is not to say that biblical interpretation is open to any fanciful flight of the imagination. Interpretation remains interpretation of *the text*. The shared, communal dimensions of their faith experience provided the biblical authors with the limits which controlled their description of revealed truths. The biblical text which we possess helps delimit the parameters for our own apprehension of revelation. Nevertheless, the ways in which the biblical authors perceived themselves and their world (largely a personal and creative enterprise) affected the ways in which they construed God's mode of presence in that world. These presuppositions or world view gave them the particular perspectives from which they could apprehend and formulate their revealed truths. Likewise, our own self-perceptions, largely imaginative in the sense of being personal and deeper than simple logic, affect the ways in which we construe God's presence. These presuppositions or world view influence the ways in which we experience the revelation of the biblical text.

Recognition of Presuppositions or World View

The previous CBA task force sought, among other things, to bring to conscious reflection some aspects of a particular set of presuppositions or a world view that seems operative especially in reading the Bible for ethics.[5] The hope of the study group was that explicit examination of these images may clarify hidden presuppositions of many who read the Bible for Christian ethics and may help make more precise how the Bible is normative for Christian ethics. The study group found it helpful to speak of the Christian community not so much as a depository of doctrinal statements than as a living organism. In this world view God's mode of presence is presupposed as active and dynamic rather than simply as notional and static. God is present in the Church as agent much more than as revealed ideas. God does not leave concepts or abstract truths *about* divine self so much as providing *that very* self as personal presence in community and in history.

The biblical authors seemed to work out of that presupposition in much of their writing, and it is often a presupposition of the Christian community which sees God using Scripture in the Church continuously to render a divine presence. In other words the Bible seems best approached for ethics not so much to obtain concepts and ideas, as to encounter God as agent in history. The Bible is predominantly narrative or story.[6] Much of the ethical material of the Bible is in the context of story and must not be divorced from the story, i.e., must not be reduced to abstract ethical norm or truth. (This does not intend to eliminate biblical law codes, but sees the codes as part of the story: they express the community's spirit-inspired responses to stories and reflect the values contained in the stories.)

If the Bible operates predominantly as story, then the revelation which it offers comes through the images and symbols which it evokes. It matters not only *what* the text says but *how* the text says it. The narrative element of the biblical text contains the world view of the biblical author and the context which gives ultimate meaning to the individual statements, ethical or otherwise, within the narrative. Moreover, our own presupposed world view, shaped by our present faith experience of God's presence, influences the way in which we evoke images and symbols from the biblical text. The Bible tells *its* story in such a way that it is at the same time *our* story. There is a dialectic which operates here. Our stories and the biblical stories may sometimes conflict. In that case the Bible sets the parameters within which we may tell our story and still have it as the Christian story. Nevertheless, the creative ways in which we perceive God's agency are brought to bear on the Bible so that it expresses our story.

Such an approach and use of the Bible go beyond the current methodology of biblical scholars who are using the historical-critical approach to exegesis. Historical criticism remains a valid method and has been foundational for the CBA seminar group. However, such a method has often been presumed to be adequate by itself for exegesis, and this is an exaggeration. Historical criticism leaves one only with information on what the text meant. It is invaluable for finding the sources and origins of the text, and the meaning intended by the human author. However, it does not address the fact that a text bears meaning beyond that intended explicitly by the author. It does not make explicit the world view which is presupposed by the author, nor does it concern itself with the images and symbols that offer meaning to the reader as these images and symbols emerge from the text under the influence of the reader's world view. We may say, then, that reading the Bible as story is not against the historical-critical method, but takes the text on another level in order to experience God's presence as a living agent in the Church in history and in the present. Reading the Bible as story is one effective way of showing what the text means today.

All in all, Christian biblical ethics winds up being an art as well as a science.[7] The Christian's perception of ethical responsibility derives from inner ability to integrate and interpret and respond to the images and symbols that impinge on his or her own person in the form of the biblical and the existential Christian story. The sciences of exegesis and ethics can help explain the content which bears the images and the symbols and which becomes the textual embodiment of the presupposed world view of author and reader, but the ultimate interpretation derives from the inner ability to read the images themselves in the light of one's presupposed world view. An artist is significantly helped by learning the techniques of art, but her final work is the result of intuition, feeling and integrating vision as much as of learning the rules. In the same way, Christian biblical ethics is helped enormously by its science, but its final product is just as much a work of art.

Bridging the Gap to Ethics

The previous CBA task force not only devoted time to working within the biblical dimensions of Christian biblical ethics, but also attempted to build some bridges with ethics by working within the terminology and framework of ethicians. This is reflected in *Christian Biblical Ethics* by a survey of ethical terms and by asking the question of how the Bible is normative in reference to these terms. A final solution is not suggested, but the survey offers a number of fruitful possibilities for the link of the Bible to ethics.[8]

To begin with, what do we mean by "norm"? Ethicists usually understand a norm as a standard or measure of conduct. However, they also distinguish between theoretical norms which are more descriptive in nature and practical norms which dictate specific action. While most people seem concerned with the second kind of norm, it may be that the Bible dwells on the first kind. Perhaps especially on the level of story the Bible provides theoretical norms without functioning to bind actions directly and absolutely. Consideration must also be given to what extent norms are in any case ultimate. Some ethicists observe that norms point to values as ultimate. Values are those qualities that enhance human persons and bring them to full existence. The Bible may serve well to name values rather than to give norms. Perhaps also the Bible establishes priorities among values. Another way of stating this is to ask whether the Bible is concerned with giving principles rather than norms. In this view norms are seen as more fixed and inflexible, whereas principles admit of variation and mediate an interpretation of reality. Is it the case that when the Bible tells its story, the particular world views of biblical author and reader issue forth images and symbols which, described as principles of ethics, embody particular interpretations of life?

Another way of coming to these same realities and to a possible role of the Bible is to speak of material norms (concrete rules of action; norms as we spoke of them above) and formal norms (the theories or presuppositions that ground our actions; principles as we spoke of them above). Is the Bible, perhaps, concerned with giving us formal norms rather than material norms? Still another way of asking this question is to phrase it in other terms used by some ethicists who distinguish meta-ethics and ethics (the ground of all theory and the theory) from morals (the application of theory). In this vocabulary is the Bible more concerned with meta-ethical or ethical issues than with morals?

In all of the above considerations of terminology, the concern was in specifying the "normativity" of the Bible in some way. One final distinction of ethicists allows the question of whether "normativity" should be used at all, at least insofar as this would link the Bible to norms or principles. Ethicists distinguish commands or norms (whether general or specific) from parenesis or exhortation. Bruno Schüller has observed that when law is joined to Gospel in the biblical text it becomes parenesis.[9] It is designed not to give new ethical insight but to offer new power to put the insight into practice. When the Bible is read as story, does it offer images and symbols that move one more firmly and with more conviction to ethical responses that would have been perceived even without the specifically Christian world view and its application to the biblical text?

Such, then, are the preliminary suggestions of a recent

task force for bridging the gap between Bible and ethics and for relating what the text meant to what the text means in ethics today. It is by no means a finished study and may perhaps do no more than posit the questions and focus the issue. It demands further testing and clarification. In what follows there is an attempt to carry on that study in relation to the specific ethical concerns of war and peace.

The Present Study: Examining World Views

One of the hermeneutical observations which surface in these studies pertains to the analysis of the presupposed world views of both biblical writer and reader. How does one perceive the image of God and what are the emphases and presuppositions of the human experience within which one perceives God? If one raises to consciousness the presuppositions about human life, one discovers many world views affecting the search for the biblical message about peace. Some of the images show contrast between biblical authors, some between biblical readers. In turn, some of the images of the biblical reader show a complementarity with the presupposed world views of the biblical author, while others show contrast. Some contrasts suggest that the presuppositions of the reader should be challenged by that of the author, while other contrasts show how perspectives of the reader may derive new meaning from the text as it leaves the world of the author for new worlds. Our studies will illustrate these varied combinations, concentrating particularly on presupposed world views related to the social dimensions of human experience and their relationship to peace.

One prominent contrast surfaces between readers when they approach the biblical text with images of self-sufficiency instead of interdependence. This contrast is reflected in the debate over individualism or the need for community. All of the articles which follow begin with a presumption that human

existence is communal in nature and that an adequate definition of an individual requires some reference also to community. This assumption seems borne out by the reading of the
Bible, where the biblical authors commonly assume a communal dimension to human existence and challenge individualistic views. That is why this book refers to the *social*
foundations of peace. The presupposition is so strong that it is
the starting point for each of the chapters.

There is, nevertheless, further debate even after one accepts the self-image of interdependence within community.
The contrast in world view carries out in the different ways *the
community* experiences itself as interdependent or self-sufficient. The communal self-image operates first with reference
to the community's relationship to God. In regard to peace
studies this contrast is reflected in the presuppositions about
national sovereignty, the need for establishing one's own national security, and the confidence in western values and
achievements. Advertence to these assumptions, with some
critical distance for evaluating them, enables one to address
the Bible and to discern more clearly the presuppositions of
the biblical authors. Such discernment may challenge our presuppositions or may sustain them, but in a more qualified way.
In several following studies there surfaces the questions just
how much is peace God's work rather than humanity's and
what are the limits to the self-sufficiency and self-achievement
of nations and governments. Such questions arise, for instance, when Chapter One discusses assumptions over biblical
teaching about monarchy and holy war, or when Chapter Five
raises like concerns in treating Paul's teaching about principalities and powers. The questions surface when Chapter
Seven surveys the history of interpretation of several key texts
related to peace issues, texts like Mt 5:39 ("turn the other
cheek"), Rom 13:1 ("all authority comes from God"), and Rev
13:2 (the dragon who is Satan gives authority to the beast that
is the Roman empire).

Sometimes the contrast between interdependence and

self-sufficiency is not between community and God but between groups in society. Consciousness raised by particular marginalized groups within a society may conflict with prevailing assumptions, and may lead to modification of such assumptions. This in turn may lead to discovery of new insights from the biblical text. Chapter Two of this book pays specific attention to what happens when feminine presuppositions are allowed to come to consciousness and are related to peace issues. They may offer new insights into wisdom literature in the Bible. In similar fashion, Chapter Five works with the insights that arise when oppressed minorities exercise "ideological suspicion" and expose predominant views as subtle forms of ideologies reinforcing oppression. Perhaps such insights bring new meaning to Paul's principalities and powers.

In all that we have seen, the starting point for hermeneutical consideration is the presupposition or the world view of the reader of a biblical text. Hermeneutical method may also begin sometimes with the presupposed world view of the author. This world view may be complementary to one's own world view as reader and would encourage one to search the biblical text for teaching that finds application in the present as in the past. Chapter Four offers such considerations related to peace issues in its description of community as a community of praise in Luke. Humanity must see itself as a community called to praise of God by response to God's word. This call and response give birth to a new world of praise in which peace is the impartial gift for all nations and all peoples.

While the experience of a community of praise may find resonances of complementarity between writer and reader of a biblical text, other experiences may create more of a dialectic, i.e., a mutual influence between the writer's presuppositions and the reader's, with each being both a challenge and a complement to the other. In such cases it could be that one begins with the author's vision of human experience, but one could just as well begin with the reader's. Chapters Three and Six both concentrate on such points in their presentations. Chapter Three claims the need to distinguish the intra-community concerns that underlie Matthew's beatitude about peacemakers from our modern day concerns about peacemaking as a universal task. How does one move from a blessing on Christian "insiders" to a mission to "outsiders" as well? Chapter Six takes up consideration of the mission outward from the community, but points out the importance of distinguishing the early Christian world view as a minority within society from contemporary presuppositions and world view as part of a majority in western society. The distinctions between outsiders/insiders and minority/majority uncover the dialectic raised by biblical texts concerning teaching on peace. There is continuity but in the midst of discontinuity in the presupposed world view.

The Hermeneutic Circle and World Peace

What we have been highlighting, of course, is illustration of the hermeneutic circle in biblical interpretation. The circle may be entered at any point, with entry often dictated by particular circumstances at the time of reading of the Bible. One may begin with assumptions of the reader and see how these emphasize certain views of human life and influence what one asks of the biblical teaching on peace. One may begin with the biblical teaching, analyzed within the historical and social setting of the author, and see how this helps form one's idea about peace in the world. Whichever the starting point of the circle, the interplay between author, text and reader will lead to reciprocity and mutuality of influences and effects. What the author brings to the text will form, change and/or qualify the reader's world and vision. What the reader assumes and seeks will find support in the text and/or lead to new discoveries in the text and/or be criticized and rejected by the text. The hermeneutic circle is an on-going and dynamic process. The following chapters offer illustration of the circle from varied points of entry and varied dimensions of the interplay between author, text and reader on the issue of peace.

As one embraces presuppositions about human experience, one forms along with them varied images of God encountered within these human experiences. Thus, the following articles, which try to raise consciousness about the author's or reader's presuppositions about human life, also focus on particular images of God, whether explicitly or implicitly. Among the images, we see some concentrating on God as Creator, others on God as Redeemer, and still others on God as Judge, although all articles eventually incorporate multiple images in their development. One point regarding all the imagery of God is that it tends to present God as living agent or an experienced presence in some way. The imagery is not so much an instrument for intellectual concepts of God or static truths. Story figures prominently as the vehicle through which the images come alive, whether gospel stories, parables, myths, Old Testament accounts of history or symbols of Lady Wisdom or apocalyptic powers.

We may say of this imagery that it intends to convey ethical material on all levels and to bring the Bible to bear on ethical concerns all along the way of the ethical process. Some of the chapters emphasize values and exhortation, while others dwell more on norms or principles of action relating to peace. All are conscious of the difficulty of moving from "what the text meant" to "what the text means," but all are interested in showing the contribution of the biblical material to the complicated ethical concerns of peace today.

Finally, in what follows we have not an exhaustive treatment of biblical perspectives on the social foundations of peace. We have, rather, representative treatment to illustrate hermeneutical approaches to the Bible concerning peace. Our sampling gives varied dimensions of community and God's involvement in it for the work of peace. Our sampling draws on a cross-section of biblical material, giving illustration from the Old Testament historical and wisdom literature, from Matthew and Luke's gospels, from Paul, and from the history of biblical interpretation in the Fathers and in later centuries. The hope of this CBA task force study is that the samplings offered will raise consciousness about presuppositions brought to ethical discussions and particularly peace study, will encourage a fitting use of the Bible for ethics and especially for peace issues, and will make a small contribution to the ongoing Christian teaching of the way to peace.

NOTES

1 Robert J. Daly, S.J. et al., *Christian Biblical Ethics. From Biblical Revelation to Contemporary Christian Praxis: Method and Content* (New York: Paulist Press, 1984).

2 Bruce C. Birch and Larry L. Rasmussen, *Bible and Ethics in the Christian Life* (Minneapolis: Augsburg Publishing House, 1976), pp. 15–29.

3 Daly, p. 14.

4 David H. Kelsey, *The Uses of Scripture in Recent Theology* (Philadelphia: Fortress Press, 1975).

5 The paradigm was one of those suggested by Kelsey in the work which has been cited. See Kelsey, pp. 32–55.

6 Daly, pp. 156–69.

7 Ibid., pp. 114–31.

8 Ibid., pp. 74–90.

9 Bruno Schüller, S.J., "The Debate on the Specific Character of a Christian Ethics: Some Remarks," in Charles E. Curran and Richard A. McCormick, S.J., eds., *Readings in Moral Theology No. 2: The Distinctiveness of Christian Ethics* (New York: Paulist Press, 1980), pp. 207–33.

Chapter One

WAR AND PEACE: A METHODOLOGICAL CONSIDERATION

. . . . . .

James A. Fischer, C.M.

Introduction

In 1970 James M. Gustafson wrote "The Place of Scripture in Christian Ethics: A Methodological Study."[1] It was an honest analysis of how we actually use Scripture in reaching moral decisions, using the then current invasion of Cambodia during the Vietnam war as an example. Gustafson outlined four ways in which Scripture was used in such a judgment:

1. Those actions of persons or groups which violate the *moral law* revealed in the Scripture are to be judged morally wrong.

2. Those actions of persons or groups which fall short of the *moral ideals* given in Scripture are to be judged morally wrong, or at least morally deficient.

3. Those actions of persons or groups are judged morally wrong which are *similar to* actions that are judged to be wrong or against God's will under similar circumstances in Scripture, *or* are *discordant with* actions judged to be right or in accord with God's will in Scripture.

4. Scripture witnesses to a great variety of moral values, moral norms and principles through many different kinds of biblical literature, moral laws, visions of the future, historical events, moral precepts, paranetic instruction, parables, dialogues, wisdom sayings, allegories. They are not in a simple way reducible to a single theme; rather they are directed to

particular historical contexts. The Christian community judges the actions of persons and groups to be morally wrong, or at least deficient, on the basis of reflective discourse about present events *in the light of* appeals to this variety of materials as well as to other principles and experiences.

Gustafson judged that the fourth alternative was the most honest approach albeit the most difficult. The third is certainly the easiest and most used. We simply say: this is like this biblical situation, and then go on to solve the problem. One and two are simplistic and need not detain us.

In 1984 the members of the Catholic Biblical Association task force which published *Christian Biblical Ethics* explored many of these same issues with applications to a dozen or more specific problems.[2] The task force accepted implicitly the complications mentioned by Gustafson and proceeded basically on his fourth proposal, including a consideration of the later reflections and experiences of the Christian community (i.e. the contemporary state of ethics among Catholic authors). What emerged as central for it was the role played by images in human decision-making, both biblical and contemporary. Even matters which we consider as "principles" are often statements of contemporary social images.

In 1983 the present task force began commenting on the preliminary draft of the bishops' pastoral, *The Challenge of Peace*.[3] The preliminary draft in its biblical section pasted together a mélange of texts having only a superficial relationship to an honest survey. Obviously, the instructions to the biblical research people had been to put across an image of peace. The whole biblical section was completely revised for the better in the second draft to take into account the varieties of literary forms and ambiguities in which peace is discussed in the Bible. However, the conclusions had already been reached by that time and it seemed fairly clear that the biblical texts were cited not as the basis for what the bishops wanted to say but as a confirmation of the overall impression that they had already agreed upon. Their presupposed self-image or world view influenced how they read the text. Unsuspectingly the images dominated the presentation.

So also the reception of the final draft was largely governed by images. The bishops had created an image of themselves as reasonable, religious leaders who were opposed to war. They had built onto previous images.

The American Civil Religion Image

The image is so named from the source of the theory and the historical stance which Americans in public life have taken.[4] Basically, this is the just war theory of Augustine as assimilated into American culture. In the *jus ad bellum* aspect (the principles for entering into war) American civil religion has tended to expand the right to self-defense into an obligation to defend the rights of others who are threatened. Self-defense on our own territorial mass has not yet been a critical factor in American history; the defense of the freedom of others has been our most normal justification. As to *jus in bello* (the principles of behavior within a war) American civil religion does recognize the need for proportionality and discrimination in the use of force, but the boundaries we set are not so clearly perceived. Such are the justifications and they are basically acceptable. In practice we have, of course, more or less hewed to this line with a realistic emphasis on the less. But the image we have projected is of Uncle Sam as the worldwide defender of the oppressed, and if the oppression can be addressed only by war, Uncle Sam will win. We see here the predominant world view of a self-sufficient community. This picture has been marred by our recent experiences, but continues to predominate.

The moral value of this image may be compared to the self-image of pacifists on the one hand or of the USSR on the other. The former proceeds either from pragmatism or a Christian ideal of non-violence; the latter proceeds from a theory of history which dictates that communism shall bury imperialism.

Both approaches, however, are basically imaged and bring each a different presupposed world view that affects the reading of the Bible.

The Image of the National Conference of Catholic Bishops

The bishops have created a different image of themselves by going beyond the generally accepted image of American civil religion. They have done this in two ways: (1) by advocating pacifism as an authentic Christian option, and (2) by claiming that nuclear weapons by their very nature exceed the qualifications for discrimination and proportionality. They have spoken of the inadequacy of the just war theory, but thus far they seem to have adopted it as theory.

Such is the theoretical basis. The pastoral has many qualifications which allow for possession and even threatened use of nuclear weapons as long as active and determined efforts are being made to reduce nuclear stockpiles. It is not the qualifications which have created the image, however; they have been largely ignored. The initial approbation of pacifism, strongly nuanced though it be, seems to have created the first impression, and then the condemnation of specific Reagan policies for an arms build-up based on threatened use of nuclear weapons *en masse* seems to be central to the image. The bishops, however, convey the predominant world view of community dependent on God.

Methodology of CBA Task Force

The brief statement here will emphasize only the elements of the method which are emphasized in this chapter. The method presumes that most of our moral decisions are based on presupposed images that comprise a world view. Usually such images are in conflict. Christians may reach conflicting conclusions depending on which images present themselves as central. Indeed, the conflict is never entirely settled for any Christian. When the moment of decision arrives, the Christian makes a choice in faith. The faith is trust in personal honesty as well as in the goodness of a God who understands and will lead the Christian to further growth. The tradition of the biblical text and the tradition of the faith community mark the parameters of such faith. It is only at the moment of decision that an act becomes truly and spiritually moral in a Christian sense, for it is only at that moment that it is an act of faith.

Images in Conflict

The bishops have pictured themselves on the side of peace in a specific way. They indicate that they are conscious of this image making. Their Christian opponents also project an image. Few of those who immediately opposed the bishops' statement had read the pastoral letter and many seem not to have done so yet. Nonetheless, they felt threatened by it. Their world view contained, among other things, varied emphases on how dependent one was on God for peace or how self-sufficient. This was seen in the way their self-images ranged from committed pacifists to superpatriots. What is happening is not so much a dialogue as a confrontation on the basis of opposing images. The first step, therefore, should be to define the conflicting images with more accuracy.

The Question

The question which now emerges is not immediately which view is objectively correct, but how individuals and especially groups shall make a Christian decision within the conflict of images. If the Bible can shed any light on this aspect of conflict of images, then perhaps we shall have made progress toward a reasonable dialogue in which we can listen to one another. Three examples are given here which illustrate how the

Old Testament occasionally dealt with such problems which provoked conflict among the chosen people.

Biblical Examples—Monarchy and War

The first example discusses the problem created by pro- and anti-monarchial sentiments expressed in 1 Samuel 8–12, where Saul is selected as king through Samuel. The problem is political as well as theological. In the opinion of some commentators it is connected with "holy war." So we have an example which bears on our subject even if indirectly.

1 Samuel 8:1–22

This is the first of five sub-units in the story. It tells of the initial request made by the Israelite people for a king. It is anti-monarchial; in some ways the disturbing specification of the rights of the king in 8:11–17 may be the most biting anti-monarchial denunciation as well as the oldest tradition.

As a story, 1 Samuel 8 is typical of much of the Deuteronomist's problem-evoking technique. I use a rhetorical criticism method here. The characters involved are Samuel, God and the people. Samuel in the historical pre-note (8:1–3) is a judge who appoints his own sons to succeed him. He is portrayed as a somewhat foolish and selfish father who cannot face the reality that his sons are crooks and that times have changed (8:4). On the other hand, he is pictured as enough of a seer to foresee the dangers of kingship; he foretells injustice far greater than his sons could accomplish (8:11–17, the oldest source). So Samuel recovers his vision. His prophetic judgment: "on that day the Lord will not answer you" (8:18) is straight Deuteronomic judgment. It is reminiscent of Joshua's challenge in Joshua 24:19–20. Samuel is so struck with his own warning that he needs to postpone final judgment: "Each of you go to his own city" (8:22). So the prophet is pictured as a man overwhelmed by his own vision of evils to come from which there is no escape even in forgiveness. He needs time to work out his inner conflict.

God is pictured as a familiar of Samuel who speaks immediately to the prophet and straight from the shoulder. God's instructions are precise but paradoxical. Although God had agreed with the prophet that the people had rejected both of them, the instruction was: "Grant the people's every request" (8:6). God knows the people's sin and, in the later Samuel speech noted above, says God will not answer their cries.

The people are pictured as taking the initiative in demanding a king and in refusing to take no for an answer. They must have a king like the other nations. They have no inner conflict, but they are in conflict with Samuel.

This introduces the final important image, that of the king. The descriptions given in 1 Samuel 8 are based on the Canaanite city-king. He is the warlord with his army of nobles who earns his position of power and opulence (8:11–18) by defending the agricultural countryside. The king at the end of the story stands in contrast to the judge (Samuel) at the beginning. Samuel had no standing army; he had no city of his own, but apparently presided at a cult shrine (Mispah?) which belonged to the tribes. The people were victimized in both cases; Samuel's sons sought illicit gain and accepted bribes (8:3); the king's oppression will be legalized and institutionalized (8:11–18).

The conflict of images between Samuel and the people is over the picture of the king desired. The people want a local warlord; Samuel and God don't want the people to put their trust in such a king. The community must show more interdependence with God in its work and the king is seen as a symbol of self-sufficient competition to God and the abdication of community responsibility.

1 Samuel 9:1–10:16

The second sub-unit is the story of how Samuel came to anoint the boy Saul. The basic source seems to be an ancient folktale of how "a young man in search of asses found a kingdom." With this has been joined a "call narrative" for a prophet. Presumably, the verses dealing with Saul in a prophetic setting were added by northern prophetic circles (e.g. 9:15–17, 21; 10:5–7 at least). 1 Sam 10:10–12 adds an etiological story explaining the proverb: "Is Saul also among the prophets?"

Both the folktale and the later additions cast Saul in the role of a prophet who is under the direction of the spirit. The warlord image has been replaced by the judge image. Yet there is a secretiveness about the whole affair. Saul's family must not know where he has been and his route is deliberately confusing. His future is uncertain. The plot builds tension by deliberate slowing down of the action. Waiting for the spirit to act seems to be characteristic of the technique. The prophet image and the judge image are being played off one against the other, but in both there is a world view of a community with a king who can function in positive fashion in relationship to God.

The Dynamism of Conflicting Images

Source and form criticism can confuse the overall rhetorical pattern in 1 Samuel 8–12. We have looked at only two of the stories; in the canonical text all five stories are a unity. The story begins with the rejection of Samuel's sons as judges in 8:1–5; the story ends (12:1–5) with a challenge to the people to recognize Samuel's integrity. Against this beginning and end is set the story of Saul: how much integrity will he have?

Similarly the "They have not rejected you, but me" speech in 1 Samuel 8:7 is paralleled by the traditional account of how the people were willing to accept divinely sent deliv-

erers from Moses to Samson, but then changed when Nahash,
the king of the Ammonites, threatened them (12:12). Only the
conclusion is the same (12:17) as the beginning: "Thus you
will see and understand how greatly the Lord is displeased that
you have asked for a king."

Dennis McCarthy has contended that 1 Samuel 12 is the
solution to the interleafed anti- and pro-monarchial sources.[5]
The people seem to repent. Unfortunately, the story as story
does not say they did. The people admit their sin in asking for
a king (12:19), but they do not desist. God is caught because
God cannot disavow the people whom the Almighty has chosen (12:22): Samuel cannot give up praying for them (12:23).
But neither does the sinfulness stop. The prophetic message
is not the "if" of a conditional covenant, but the inevitability
of destruction. The story is a tragedy, not an heroic vision of
the future. Nothing has been added to the image of the king;
he is still the warlord who will fatten on the people and lack
integrity. The people are still the people who want a king like
other nations. The oddity is that God can tolerate it—as long
as they fear the Lord and worship God faithfully (12:24).

Trajectory

It is, of course, hazardous to attempt trajectories. But
some things are clear even from this brief survey. The prophet
image stands out. Moses was remembered principally as a
prophet and Joshua succeeded him as a prophet. The judges
were indeed military saviors, but generally they were led by
the Spirit or a prophet or prophetess. The role of the prophet
in the Book of Judges slowly dies out in the present arrangement of the text. 1 Samuel begins with a restoration of emphasis on prophecy, but that fades quickly.

There is a later attempt to go back to prophetic leadership. After Saul David, too, is found among the prophets (1
Sam 19:18–21) and earns a traditional reputation as a prophet,
especially as composer of psalms. But after David prophecy is

no longer connected with kings. In the Deuteronomist's final denunciation of the kingdom of Israel (2 Kgs 17:7–23) the lack of dependence on prophets is the principal criticism.

So if we ask what the conflict was all about, the stories indicate that it centered on the inclusion or exclusion of the image of prophet within the image of the king. And this is connected with the ethics of every Israelite. If there is something of truth in Mendenhall's contention, the exodus was not simply liberation from an *ad hoc* oppression, but from all forms of authoritarian government. What the exodus did was to liberate an ethical revolution which placed responsibility for community welfare on each individual. This is the prophet's role.

> The ethic had predictive value—in fact, the ethic consisted in large part of the ability of persons to predict the consequences of their behavior as they affected other persons and caused them to react. This is one of the foundations of pre-Exilic prophecy, which enabled them to predict the course of history with uncanny accuracy.
>
> The prophetic message is relatively simple: the rejection of those ethical controls that were identified with the rule of God constituted the rejection of God Himself, and therefore the corporate existence brought about by that divine rule could no longer be legitimized by appeal to Yahweh. On the contrary, it must be destroyed as the enemy of Yahweh.[6]

The community was not dependent on God, but proud in its abdication of power and responsibility to a self-sufficient king.

What Mendenhall is saying fits the overall story element of Deuteronomy's history as accepted in its canonical form. Its story of the monarchy is a tragedy and a predictable one at that. Davidic kingship is not the solution; what was positive in David's kingship was the exception. In general the "king as the other nations have" was the primitive request and the abiding reality.

Yet the picture of the king did persist and in a way that was acceptable even in tension. It led to a totally different picture of what was involved. The ethical revolution of the exodus did place responsibility for the community on each individual, so that the image and the function of a king was altered. The kingly mantle and the prophetic spirit fell on all the people (cf. Ex 19:6 and Num 11:29) and this important tradition was taken up in the New Testament (cf. 1 Pet 2:9 and Acts 2:17–18 among others). The king was in reality the Everyman—as was Christ. So I have argued elsewhere.[7] The Jeremian statement on the new covenant is decisive in this direction (Jer 31:31–34).[8] The reconciliation was not on theoretic or logical lines, but on story lines which united the conflicting images in a Person. Kingship could be seen in some positive light only as divorced from images of self-reliance competitive to God and as part of a community all of whose members lived with a sense of interdependence with God in doing God's work.

Holy War and Prophetic Peace

"Holy war" is not a biblical term but one which we have invented for our own interpretation.[9] The biblical term is *herem*, "dedicated." It first appears in the story of the destruction of Jericho (cf. Jos 1:18 and the associated story of Achan in Jos 7:1, 11, 13, 15) to designate that which should have been dedicated totally to God. It is not part of a report; as far as we can tell historically, the Israelites were nowhere near Jericho geographically or chronologically when it was destroyed. The word is an interpretation from a later age which explains something about the significance of the destruction, not about what the Lord commanded the Israelites to do.

So also Saul's campaign against Amalek is described in 1 Samuel 15 as *herem* and the word is used in v. 20 as part of Saul's self-justification. Source criticism is quite uncertain about the provenance or antiquity of this story.[10] However, it is generally agreed that the source was from prophetic circles and already contained a prophetic judgment. In other words, we don't know much about the historicity of what happened in the Amalek incident, but we do know that in prophetic interpretation the story made the point that the prophets had to be obeyed. Later writers looking back on such an event could either attribute a total victory to the Lord and so say that God had decreed and accomplished *herem* or they could see that the victory was only partial and so blame the proclaimed human victor for violating the ban. So for Jericho and so for Saul.

Herem and Holy War

It is obvious that the concept of divine approval for total destruction is a very helpful one for any military government. The kings of Judah and Israel are notable for the wars they waged, even if they were minuscule. Nowhere are these designated as "holy wars" in any sense; indeed, they are mostly denounced by the prophets as self-serving or self-sufficient. Nonetheless, the concept of God the Warrior is strong in the Old Testament, nowhere more so than in the poetic pieces as ancient as the Song of the Sea (Ex 15) or the Psalms. The late apocalyptic literature is fueled by the concept of God the Warrior who scores the total victory. *All of this was not intended to glorify actual warfare nor to give a moral norm, but to teach that any worthwhile victory belongs to God alone.* It continues into the New Testament in the minor apocalypses and the pictures of the super-mundane Christ in Paul, not to mention Revelation.

In other words, considering the redactional context of the concepts of *herem, war is not holy because God commanded it; it is holy only in the sense that the victory is totally ascribed to God.* In one of those mind-shattering sayings about repentance, God is said to have repented that God made Saul king (1 Sam 15:35; cf. also Gen 6:6; Ex 32:14; 2 Sam 24:16; Jer 18:8; Am 7:3; Jon 3:10 for other repentances of God). God lost; the war against Amalek was not holy. Presumably the possibility existed that the war might have been called holy if Saul had obeyed. Later generations could derive no profit from calling it such.

Within the narrative tradition the glorious things which were said of the king do not come from his proven ability as a warlord, but from his total dependence on God. The Nathan prophecy of sonship for the king is simply a continuation of the choice of the seed of Abraham and of the exodus people. They are to be witnesses to the power and "holiness" of God. Whatever victories they win—and there were relatively few of them—simply attest to the power of God. So in the later Isaian prophecies, both proto- and deutero-Isaiah, the warlord characteristics of the king are suppressed and the Child or Servant image dominates. Warmaking as such becomes irrelevant except as the imagery defines the supreme dominion of God. In some of the most bloodthirsty passages in the Bible the prophets describe the destruction of traditional enemies from Ammonites to Assyrians. The prophets shift the "holy war" imagery to a cosmic and divine sphere. "Peace" is always a gift which is not only given, but which God in God's own time will make prevail.

This conflicting imagery which centers on God the Warrior and God the Peacemaker simply reflects the confusing choices which faced the people who had to make choices in specific situations. It was for them to choose whether a specific situation called for standing up for justice and fighting or for waiting through persecution for God to vindicate the just. The only constant is the admission that whatever one does, it must be done with full recognition that only God can see one through the crisis. The moral question becomes one of honesty in assessing one's motives or self-images. War and peace are emotional issues in which honesty is sorely tried. There is no clear and universal imperative as to whether one should fight or be quiet. The faith called forth by persecution may be no greater nor less than the faith called forth by war. After all, the tradition has canonized Maccabees and Esther as well as Isaiah, and we should now turn to these briefly.

Maccabees

Jonathan Goldstein in his Anchor Bible Commentaries on 1 and 2 Maccabees contends that 1 Maccabees represents the war party and 2 Maccabees the pro-pacifism (or submission) temple propaganda for the same war. Relatively few authors have commented recently on 1 and 2 Maccabees, so our critical base is limited.[11]

Basic Argument

"These two books present sharply different accounts; indeed, we shall find that their authors were bitter opponents."[12] In analyzing 1 Maccabees, Goldstein puts most emphasis on chapter two, the story of the revolt of Matthathias, which he sees as a deliberate editorial creation casting Matthathias as a new Phineas. Then he emphasizes the centrality of the decision to fight on the sabbath as a compromise position defending Torah by violating Torah. As the story continues, it really becomes the story of the Hasmonaeans (which Goldstein thinks was the original title of the book from Matthathias' second name: Hashmonay). There is no prophecy nor any attempt to say that prophecy is fulfilled; there are no miracles. Yet the author of Maccabees hints broadly that the Hasmonaeans are legitimate as the fulfillers of prophecy. Like earlier Old Testament histories, 1 Maccabees used a chronological framework; it is relatively sober and accurate.

2 Maccabees is entirely different, a summary of the five books of Jason, which tells the story of the rededication of the temple in 165 B.C. and never mentions Matthathias. After the two introductory letters which are somewhat irrelevant, it begins with the pious priest Onias III defying Heliodorus and being delivered by angel guards. There are differences between 1 Maccabees and 2 Maccabees in the stories which are selected to tell of how events led up to the purification of the Temple. The contrasts of Jason's work with 1 Maccabees go

far beyond miracles and other details of narrative. Where 1 Maccabees was written to prove the legitimacy of the Hasmonaean dynasty, Jason pointedly makes every effort to show that Judas' brothers were at best ineffective and at worst tainted by treason and sin. Where in 1 Maccabees there is strong, if tacit, denial of the resurrection, Jason loudly asserts the belief (2 Macc 7; 14:46) and goes through logical gymnastics to prove that Judas himself held it (2 Macc 12:42–45). Where in 1 Maccabees, without obedience to the Hasmonaeans, piety and even martyrdom are not enough to win God's favor, Jason makes even Judas' victories a result of divine favor won by the martyrs. Where in 1 Maccabees the commemorative festivals, the Feast of Dedication and the Day of Nicanor, are mentioned, they do not become the focus of attention; in 2 Maccabees and perhaps in the complete work of Jason the narrative is organized in two parallel sections, each telling of threat to the temple, martyrdom, triumph, with the first celebration of each festival as the climax.[13] There is only a tenuous chronological framework here—only two dates are mentioned in 2 Maccabees. So Goldstein considers 2 Maccabees a cultic text, not a "pathetic history."

Critique of Goldstein

Let us grant for the sake of argument that this is a reasonable analysis of two divergent views of the same war. The central question would be: Why did the Jewish community preserve the divergent texts and why did the Alexandrian community and the later Christian community canonize as inspired two divergent views? We do not have any studies on this point. Goldstein has only a brief note that

> The Church Fathers were inspired by the tales of the courage of the defenders of the faith [i.e., in 1 Macc]. The pietistic teachings of Second Maccabees probably led them to expect similar views from our author, so that they failed to perceive his drastic but tacit denial of the resurrection.

> Hence, though Jews ceased to preserve First Maccabees,
> the Church treasured the Greek version and from it made
> others in Latin, Syriac, and Aramenian.[14]

And: "Hence, although the theology of Second Maccabees was so acceptable to Jews that martyr tales in rabbinic literature are probably influenced by it, the book was preserved only by the Church. Medieval Jews were glad to draw on its narrative for inspiration when they rediscovered it in the possession of their Christian contemporaries."[15]

Conclusion

Goldstein seems to have made a fair argument for his analysis. The weak point is why the Palestinian-MT tradition did not accept both Maccabee books and the Alexandrian-Christian tradition did. Certainly the evidence that 2 Maccabees was esteemed because of the martyr stories is very thin and unconvincing. It must be remembered that the so-called canonizing at Jamnia was done by a Pharisee sect which was still embroiled, as it had been for years, in the argument over the proper attitude toward the conquerors and was inclined to the pacifism side. It would seem, at least, that those scholars were still divided and could not reach a consensus on either attitude represented by the two Maccabee books. On the other hand, the Alexandrian tradition was not so concerned about such immediate political matters; they had made their peace with the conquerors. I suspect that the Fathers accepted both Maccabees for the same reason the Council of Trent accepted them—namely, tradition. The tradition had come down to them in the Alexandrian form and that was all that was required. They certainly were not adopted as an ethical norm.

Esther

A third example dealing with a war and peace issue is Esther. The topic discussed is a pogrom and a preventive war.

The Canonical Problem

Hebrew Esther is somewhat of an embarrassment in the Hebrew Old Testament canon. The core thesis is the story of a pogrom which was averted by a preventive riot in which the Jews killed many of their enemies. Jewish commentators are concerned to justify why this story was considered "word of God."

There are extenuating circumstances, of course. One may say that the book is not historical, that the numbers of the slain are probably exaggerated and that they were not very large in any case. Or with Robert Gordis one may interpret Esther 8:11 to limit the enmity to Haman.[16] There is something to be said for all these views and for others. One may say that the thesis of the book is not the slaughter, but the Feast of Purim which is connected with the story. It may be said that the theme is the action of God and the slaughter is no more blood-curdling than the exodus story on which some commentators think the story is modeled.[17] However, that leaves the story as the justification for the feast and this may be contested historically. It may be said that the Jews were much more restrained and considerate of others than at first appears. That may be true. But the story does say that they killed some people who were not ready to defend themselves. The tradition accepted this. It certainly cannot be defended as an open and shut case of Jewish self-defense.

Robert Gordis probably has the Jewish viewpoint expressed best. He simply concludes at the end that anything which preserves the chosen people is justified since that was God's radical purpose. The explanation is not as self-serving and chauvinistic as it sounds. It is not a whitewash for the people who planned and carried out the operation. It is an understanding from a later time which struggled with the fact or fiction that such and such had happened. How could God allow this? Or do it? The Hebrew text simply implies that it was always God's plan to save the people. On that basis the story and the annexed cultic traditions were preserved.

However, there is a minority report on file. The Greek translation adds a prologue-epilogue, several prayers and a few extra documents.[18] For our purpose it is the prologue-epilogue which is to the point. They are in the literary form of a dream technique.[19] That technique tells us that the author knows something which the *personae dramatis* do not. In the epilogue Haman and Mordecai are both seen as terrible dragons. The interpretation of the story has shifted from triumphalism to acknowledgment that the human activity has gone astray. Esther and God still remain heroes; Mordecai has changed into an anti-hero. That is the form in which the complete story was accepted by the Greek editors and later canonized by the Christian community.

We know nothing about the subsequent history of the canonizing process in this instance except what we can deduce from the Hebrew and the Greek texts. How these additions originated or what theological party is represented by them cannot be determined. The opinion seems fairly well divided between an Alexandrine and a Palestinian origin for the additions with the dominant side leaning toward the Egyptian explanation. Although there is a good deal of rabbinic commentary and justification for the Hebrew version, we have no comment at all from that source on the Greek additions. Even the meager patristic comment from the Christian side is limited to the Hebrew story itself apart from the Greek additions.[20]

It is interesting to note how historical critics deal with this problem; they simply dismiss the Greek additions as unimportant and even uninteresting.[21] They yield no historical data and so they are considered valueless. From a rhetorical criticism viewpoint, however, the exact opposite seems true. The total story as story does disclose some theological intent.

Dream sequences are commonly used in the Old Testament to allow the author to give his own interpretation of a story. In this case the author has used a quasi-apocalyptic vision involving dragons, a woman and a river. The dragon is a completely understandable figure. In the epilogue the surprise factor occurs when both Haman, the obvious villain, and Mordecai, the hero, are identified with the dragons. In the case of Mordecai this is a typical role reversal plot.

James Loader has analyzed the story in the Hebrew version on three levels.[22] On level one we have a hero story about Mordecai, the principal actor, and Esther, who is controlled by him. They succeed by intrigue in averting the evil fate of their people and of taking a triumphalistic revenge. The story is the setting for the Feast of Purim and from very early times it was read at the feast. On the second level the Hebrew text is the story of God, who is not mentioned at all, acting much as God did in the exodus story (so the exodus archetype). So an interpretation of God's salvific will for this chosen people is legitimate on this level. On the third level the story is one of human psychology. Mordecai acts out of his own initiatives and achieves his end, but it is really the concealed God who acts. A number of biblical stories are told which are seemingly secular in nature, but which are really about the God who conceals self. In Loader's explanation the first two levels conform rather well to standard criticism, but the theme of the "concealed God" is unique.

Going beyond Loader it may be pointed out that the Greek additions simply made the action of the "concealed God" apparent. Part of this was done rather baldly by adding various prayers. The really artistic twist, however, was added by the prologue-epilogue. Obviously this is an envelope technique which is intended to be the guiding interpretative element.[23]

Now if this be so, we have a story about deliberate bloodshed which has two divergent interpretations. The ethical judgment is not about an action to be performed since the story is of events past. Nor is it presented as an exemplar for future actions, although it may have incited participants in the feast to that attitude in later times. As many commentators have observed, the whole story has a tinge of wisdom thinking about it. It is a reflection on what has happened, whether fictional or real makes no difference. The author or editors are trying to see the hand of God behind the images in the story they are telling—otherwise the book would not have been accepted as canonical or sacred by anyone. But one author says it one way and another quite differently.

Conclusions to the Whole Study

Other examples might well be cited from the Old Testament, not only from story form but from the legal prescriptions in Deuteronomy concerning "holy war," which were perfected long after there was any opportunity for waging war of any sort. We could also adduce conflicting attitudes from the Psalms, etc. However, there is enough here to make some tentative conclusions.

1. The rhetorical intent of the material we have studied was to reflect upon the past and see God present in events, not to make normative statements for the future. The stories took images in conflict and discovered something behind them which was more important.
2. The reflection is intended to uncover the hand of God mostly in traditional stories. It did not seem to matter a great deal whether the stories were pro-war or pro-peace or for that matter whether they were considered factual or fictional.
3. The problem with diagnosing New Testament ethics about war is that we are tempted to find an ethical principle which is obligatory. If the Sermon on the Mount in Matthew, for example, is interpreted as leading to some sort of principle of non-violence, called either precept or counsel, then we are dealing with a quite different approach than we had in the Old Testament. However, the key text in Matthew is

5:48 which is obviously a version of Dt 18:13 and/or Lev
19:2. It enjoins the imitation of God without telling us just
how God would act. It gives us images of good and bad people acting and asks: "Is that the way God would act?" I
think it is undoubtedly true that the New Testament leans
toward the side of peace and non-violence. But it doesn't
make an obligatory ethic of it. If so, God the Warrior is in
bad shape.

   That peace is a good which we should desire and do what
we can to obtain seems self-evident. One does not need to be
a Christian to arrive at that conclusion. That peace is not often
within our own power to achieve seems to be common sense
observation on human history. That we may hinder or help
peace by our concerns for justice seems to be a fairly clear proposal both to imperialists and communists and others. How it
is to be obtained in specific circumstances is where we differ.
The human perceptions of how we should act on the conflicting images is the basis of our disagreement. Behind this conflict is a more fundamental one about the nature of any of the
conflicting images. We are still tempted to think that the question is whether we should make war or make peace—in other
words, on which side we should be the heroes. Neither solution is really in our hands. We may be dealing with a comedy.
The prospects of nuclear conflict are clear enough to warn us
that the danger is that the situation will simply get out of hand.
So also is peace. The fundamental flaw on both sides is in
thinking that we are in control. Only when we come to consider the possibility that human life may be a comedy do we
give room for an inbreaking of the supra-rational power of God.
Pacifism may be as vicious as militarism. The desire to conquer may vitiate heroism in either field.

NOTES
..

1 James M. Gustafson, "The Place of Scripture in Christian Ethics: A Methodological Study," *Interpretation* 24 (1970):430–45.

2 Robert J. Daly, S.J. et al., *Christian Biblical Ethics. From Biblical Revelation to Contemporary Christian Praxis: Method and Content* (New York: Paulist Press, 1984). Cf. particularly the summary of methodology on pp. 289–95.

3 National Conference of Catholic Bishops, *The Challenge of Peace: God's Promise and Our Response,* third draft (Washington, D.C.: United States Catholic Conference, 1983).

4 Barry Smernoff, "An Exploratory Moral Analysis of Strategic Nuclear Options and Arms-control Regimes," *Military Chaplains Review* (1982):45–76. It may seem somewhat strange to find an extremely well-balanced presentation on war in a military review, but so it is.

5 Dennis J. McCarthy, "The Inauguration of the Monarchy in Israel," *Interpretation* 27 (1973):401–412.

6 George E. Mendenhall, *The Tenth Generation* (Baltimore: Johns Hopkins, 1973), p. 30.

7 James A. Fischer, "Everyone a King: A Study of the Psalms," *The Bible Today* 97 (1978):1683–89.

8 John Bright, *Jeremiah,* The Anchor Bible, vol. 21 (Garden City, N.Y.: Doubleday, 1965), pp. cxiv-v.

9 Luis Alonso Schökel, *The Inspired Word* (New York: Herder and Herder, 1965), p. 156, points out the multiple meanings and emotional impact of the word.

10 Brevard Childs, *Introduction to the Old Testament as Scripture* (Philadelphia: Fortress, 1979), pp. 268–71, has a good overall survey of the state of source criticism in 1 and 2 Samuel; Bruce C. Birch, *The Rise of the Israelite Monarchy,* Society of Biblical Literature Dissertation Series, vol. 17 (Decatur: Scholars Press, 1976), pp. 94–108, has a more specific treatment of chapter 15.

11 Jonathan Goldstein, *I Maccabees,* Anchor Bible, vol. 41 (New York: Doubleday, 1976), and *II Maccabees,* Anchor Bible, vol. 41A (New

York: Doubleday, 1983); Robert Doran, *Temple Propaganda: The Purpose and Character of 2 Maccabees*, Catholic Biblical Quarterly Monograph Series, no. 12 (Washington, D.C.: Catholic Biblical Association of America, 1981); "Studies in the Style and Literary Character of 2 Maccabees," *Hebrew Union College Annual* 50 (1979):107–114, and diss. abs. in *Harvard Theological Review* 71 (1978):317; "Parties and Politics in Pre-Hasmonean Jerusalem," Society of Biblical Literature Seminar Papers, no. 21 (Decatur: Scholars Press, 1982), pp. 107–111; Elias J. Bickerman, *The God of the Maccabees* (Leiden: Brill, 1979); *Studies in Jewish and Christian History*, parts I and II, Arbeiten zur Geschichte des Antiken Judentums und des Urchristentums, Band IX (Leiden: Brill, 1976–1980); Sidney Tedesche and Solomon Zeitlin, *The First Book of Maccabees* (New York: Harper, 1950).

12 Goldstein, *1 Maccabees*, p. 33.

13 Ibid. p. 26.

14 Ibid.

15 Ibid. p. 36.

16 Robert Gordis, "Studies in the Esther Narrative," *Journal of Biblical Literature* 95 (1976):43–58.

17 James Loader, "Esther as a Novel with Different Levels of Meaning," *Zeitschrift für die alttestamentliche Wissenschaft* 90 (1978):417–21, and Charles Miller, "Esther's Levels of Meaning," *Zeitschrift für die alttestamentliche Wissenschaft* 92 (1980):145–48.

18 The additions are designated Chapters A-F in the *New American Bible*. Sometimes they are simply numbered along with the Hebrew text to produce sixteen chapters instead of ten.

19 Robert Alter, *The Art of Biblical Narrative* (New York: Basic Books, 1981), pp. 183–85.

20 J.A.F. Gregg, "Esther," in R.H. Charles, ed., *The Apocrypha and Pseudepigrapha of the Old Testament in English*, vol. I (Oxford: Clarendon, 1913), pp. 665–84.

21 Charles Cutler Torrey, *The Apocryphal Literature* (London: Archon, 1963), pp. 57–59; W.O.E. Oesterley, *An Introduction to the Books of the Apocrypha* (London: SPCK, 1958).

22 Loader, "Esther as a Novel."

23 Roland Murphy, *Wisdom Literature*, The Forms of the Old Testament Literature, vol. xiii (Grand Rapids: Eerdmans, 1981), pp. 151–71.

Chapter Two

WISDOM LITERATURE, WOMEN'S CULTURE AND PEACE: A HERMENEUTICAL REFLECTION*

. . . . . .

Kathleen M. O'Connor

Introduction

What motivates human decision and gives energy to ethical choice? What persuades people that an orientation toward life is wrongheaded or that another stance toward reality is desirable? The authors of *Christian Biblical Ethics*[1] reply that the basic myths of a society shape the consciousness, the decisions and the behaviors both of groups and of individuals. Myths are stories human communities tell about themselves to convey the distinctive meaning of their world—or their world view. These myths show the presuppositions which set the boundaries of the group's identity and of their judgments of their life and action.[2] Because myths create a symbolic world that appeals to the whole person, to emotion and imagination, as well as to reason, they evoke the vicarious participation of the community. Both consciously and unconsciously a people's myths influence their behavior.

The significance of these observations for peace studies

*I would like to acknowledge and to express appreciation to the members of Women in Theology, Ossining, New York, for their critical interaction with my work.

is that peace is unlikely, if not impossible, where a mythology of domination, violence and war prevails in the culture. Consider, for example, the power of the cowboy, the football player, the frontiersman, and now Rambo, in forming and articulating the collective consciousness of the United States. Each of these mythical figures is individualistic, competitive, and ready to use violence to solve conflicts.[3] Deeply embedded in our national consciousness, they contribute to a mythology of domination and subordination, and they create in us a propensity for war, not peace.

For ethical life to change mythology must change, and the world view which it expresses.[4] Our patriarchal mythology of domination and subordination must be transformed by a new mythology of communion and compassion, that is, by a mythology with the power to alter our understandings of human and global relations and to predispose us toward peace. This process of creating a new mythology I call the "remythologizing" of culture. To remythologize means to call forth from the common experiences and traditions of a people new mythical visions to meet a particular crisis. For instance, in the eighth century B.C.E., the prophet Hosea created a new mythology to meet the threat of Baalism when he presented Yahweh as a fertility God who transcends the cycles of the seasons and enters into historical covenant relations with Israel.

It is the thesis of this paper that two resources for a mythology of peace are already available to us, the emerging culture of women and the wisdom literature of the Old Testament. This paper describes some characteristics of our particular form of patriarchal culture which make just human relationships and, hence, peace impossible. It contrasts these characteristics of patriarchal culture with aspects of women's culture, ignored or downgraded in our society, that envision human relationships differently. Then it probes selected texts of the wisdom literature to describe a biblical vision of the human community correlative to that of women's culture.

Some Preliminary Distinctions

In this paper I am not proposing that all men or all women possess the dominant traits of patriarchal or women's culture. They do not. Some women are not yet suspicious of patriarchal mythology but some men are. Some women practice "macho-masculinity" in their lives, while some men adopt perspectives and actions of women's culture. Nor am I proposing that women are better than men. Despite attempts over the centuries to exalt "feminine virtue," women are no better nor worse than men. It is simply that men are in power and that patriarchal consciousness has shaped, named and controlled the reality in which both women and men live.

Nor am I arguing that these two cultures arise from the intrinsic nature of each sex. I do not believe that women and men are the way we are for biological reasons alone. With a growing chorus of voices from various disciplines,[5] I maintain that biological differences between the sexes are significant but not determinative. They affect us but do not determine us. That is, the values and implications based on biological differences are largely the results of culture. There is one common humanity shared equally by males and females both of whom have the potential to achieve full humanity. It is important that I say these things so that it is understood that I do not see men as warmakers and women as peacemakers. As moral and political agents women have helped to maintain systems of domination and militarism, even as they have been dominated themselves.[6] Women are not less violent than men; rather women's violence is more indirect because women's historical experience has been significantly different from that of men.[7]

Patriarchal Culture

Patriarchy is a system of relationships that institutionalize male dominance. Three interlocking characteristics of patriarchal culture in the United States illustrate why it is inherently, in its very bones and muscles, violent and inclined toward war. It is implacably hierarchical, individualistic and competitive.

Patriarchy perceives people and the universe itself according to a hierarchical scheme. It arranges persons and all of reality in a pecking order, an order claimed to be established by God and inherent in nature. As the central organizational tool of patriarchy, hierarchy permeates industry, corporations, schools, families and churches. In this social arrangement human beings are radically unequal, not just for a time through an agreement to achieve a goal or to accomplish a task, but permanently, ontologically. A privileged minority controls the life, the work, even the thinking of those "under them." Rather than being joined to one another, people are set against each other. People become others, objects, less than full human beings. When a sense of connection does exist in hierarchy it is typically that of proprietorship. Connected others are "my workers," "my flock," "my assistant," "my wife," the ones over whom I have rights and to whom I have certain responsibilities of direction and protection.

Violence is inevitable in this social system, not because it organizes people unequally, but because it cements unequal and unjust relationships into place. It institutionalizes dominance of one group over others, both women and men lower in the hierarchical scheme who lack power to control their own futures and who are dependent upon the ones over them.

The patriarchal culture of the United States predisposes us toward war also because it glorifies the individual and it idolizes competition. Extreme focus on the welfare of the individual in which the individual's development and work become the paramount reality empowers the individual against the other, the group, the society. Rather than joining people together, excessive individualism separates them by breeding competition which, in turn, further isolates the individual. Of course, there is some truth in the rationale that competition brings out the best in each citizen and makes everyone strive for excellence. However, in competition only one competitor can achieve the "number one" place in the hierarchical scheme of things. To gain that worshiped position may require the exercise of violence. It may force the suppression of much of the individual's humanity, feelings, and sense of community. The cost in human resources is extremely high. Studs Terkel illustrates the point:

> When the individual reaches the vice presidency or he's the general manager, you know he's an ambitious, dedicated guy who wants to get to the top. He isn't one of the gray people. He's one of the black and white vicious people—the leaders, the ones who stick out in a crowd. As he struggles in this jungle, in every position he's in he's terribly lonely. He can't confide and talk to the man he's working for. To give vent to his feelings, his fears, and his insecurities, he'd expose himself. This goes all the way up the line until he gets to be president. The president really doesn't have anybody to talk to, because the vice presidents are waiting for him to die or make a mistake and get knocked off so they can get the job.[8]

Just as Terkel illustrates the cost to the individual of getting to the top and staying there, similar arguments can be made regarding the nation. The effort to be the dominant superpower demands the channeling of the nation's energies into defense, into protection of honor, into security. Creative living, collaboration, and communion among groups and nations become impossible. The others must be more and more distanced, pushed back, kept at bay. Because the United States relates to other nations in the world in this way, more and more energy and money must be spent on defense so that we can be number one.

In competition, there are always losers, "also-rans," excluded from the ring of success and its rewards. In such an ethos—and this is competition's real danger—competitors become adversaries, the enemy, the dangerous other, to be "beaten," outwitted, even destroyed. In our patriarchal culture, the other is separate, distant and threatening. This is true whether we speak of competition between individuals, between ethnic and economic groups or between nations. Violence and war are inevitable.

Given these presuppositions of our culture, nothing can change. Peace, if we mean more than the occasional absence of war, needs other people, other ways of perceiving the world of relationships. Peace requires a new consciousness of the self in relation to the other and of nation in relation to nation. The midwifery of a future of peace demands new sources of life in the present. To borrow the title of an article by Dorothy Soelle, "Peace Needs Women,"[9] but not only women. Peace needs the values of women's culture.

Women's culture refers to a way of social organization which insists on the "sociality of all things."[10] It is characterized by relationships that are mutual, non-hierarchical and inclusive. Though women's culture developed in powerlessness and dependency, women are not only victims. Along with other powerless and subordinated peoples, they are practitioners of a way of relationship that could lead to a new, robust social vision, to a politics of compassion and to a predisposition toward peace.

Perhaps because women's stories are stories of the nurturance of life, or perhaps because women have been subordinated around the globe through recorded time, women's culture has developed in the womb of relationships. It is relationships that make women throb with life, squirm in discomfort, or cry out in anguish. In women's culture the other is not distant, hostile or threatening but really or potentially related.

There has been an explosion of literature on the subject of women's relationality. Two important studies offer a psychological analysis of this sense of affiliation found among women. The combined developmental works of Nancy Chodorow[11] and Carol Gilligan[12] propose that, while boys require separation from their mothers to insure male identity, girls develop in just the opposite way. To learn to be women, girls must remain identified with their mothers. The result is that boys develop a sense of autonomy, independence, a sense of self over against the other. Girls, on the contrary, never lose their sense of connectedness. It pervades female experience.

These tendencies are reinforced by the games which each sex plays in childhood. Boys' games are rule-oriented, based on justice and achievement of goals regardless of relationships among players. Girls games are process-oriented, avoiding rules, focusing on relationships. According to Gilligan, men learn to make moral decisions on the basis of abstract reasoning and independent principles of justice. They play by the rules. Women's moral decisions are based on relationships. "What effects will my decision have on my family, my friends, those whom I love?" are the operative questions.

Overemphases in both directions, independence and relationality, have created pathologies in both sexes. Only when women include the importance of their own well-being in decision-making, Gilligan argues, do their choices become adult. Similarly, only when men recognize the importance of persons, of their connections to others, do their choices attain maturity.

Objecting to the sharp dualism in Gilligan's thought between decisions based on principle and decisions based on relationships, Jean Grimshaw proposes that women's relationality arises from their historical experience as nurturers and care givers. These roles have equipped women with more principles to employ in their decision-making.[13] Grimshaw observes that women's lives often provide space for questioning cultural priorities that deny the interconnections among human beings.

Social theory offers yet another and broader way to understand women's emphasis on relationships.[14] The study of the relational behavior of oppressed groups indicates that so-called "feminine characteristics" and affiliative qualities are frequently found among subordinated peoples. Powerless individuals and groups typically place a high emphasis on personal relationships, on tact, indirection, gentleness in dealing with the dominant group. Nurturing care and emotional bonding with one's own are further survival requirements for the underclasses. These traits are, of course, two-faced, both humanizing and self-defeating. With tact comes deceit, with gentleness comes passivity, with deference for the other, self-hatred.

Whatever its source, this primary place given to relationships is typically a strength of women. Most women are relational experts. If the quality of relationship, personal, communal and global, is at the heart of peace, then the rising consciousness of women may provide ingredients for a new world view and a new mythology of peace.

Women's culture of connectedness may be an antidote to American individualism. If it is accepted that others are thinking, feeling, suffering humans, connected to us by common humanity, then there is hope for peace. When it is recognized that Nicaraguans, Russians and Iranians are also human beings like us with hopes and dreams for a decent human life, for food and shelter and dignified living, then we cannot easily do violence to them.

Women's culture is an unmined source for peace because it perceives reality communally rather than hierarchically. In women's culture no one "is over the other"; instead mutuality shapes relationships to world and people. Because women, like other powerless peoples, have been alienated from the mainstreams of life in our culture, they often strive to live in mutuality. For centuries women have explored their emotional worlds together as a tactic of survival. Perhaps this reciprocal mode of behavior partially explains why the governing principles of shared responsibility and subsidiarity, urged by the documents of Vatican II, took root among communities of religious women in a way not even palely imitated in the rest of the Church. Women's culture does not seek to conquer or surpass the other but to accept and to enhance the life of the other. Typically, women have had a profound sense of the dignity of the other. The alarming discovery among women today is that this dignity extends to women and to Afro-Americans, to Chicanos, to Puerto Ricans, to Native Americans and, indeed, to all peoples. For peace to be born, the patriarchal cultural mythology of the United States needs to be transformed and converted by women's experience, critically examined and distilled in new mythological visions.

Biblical Source

A second source for peace, correlative to the first, is the wisdom literature. Of course, women's culture cannot be equated with the wisdom literature nor with any of the biblical testimony. Nonetheless, the presuppositions and world view of women's culture influence how one reads the biblical text, provide new questions to bring to the text and yield new interpretations of the Bible on matters of peace. Before turning to the biblical text itself it is necessary to consider how the Bible functions in shaping our postures of peace and war. In what way is it normative for believers? What can it, a collection of ancient documents, tell us about peace in the twentieth century?

I begin with its limits, what the Bible is not and does not do. The Bible is not a set of laws which provide a solution to the immensely complex questions of our time. The Bible is not prescriptive. It not only fails to provide a recipe for peace; it is in conflict with itself on the question of peace. The God of the Bible is at once the God of peace and the God of war. Furthermore, even where it is not in conflict—for example, most would agree that Jesus was himself a person of peace and a non-violent resister of evil—does it automatically follow that at all times and in all circumstances, Christians must themselves follow this path exactly? This is a matter of heated debate among Christian groups, among Roman Catholic bishops and among biblical scholars. The Bible does not provide any simple or rote solution to any human problem. What the Bible does provide is the testimony of the faith community to its lived experience of God in specific historical circumstances. The Bible invites us into their stories, their images, and their worlds to challenge or to support our prevailing myths and images. The Bible functions to inspire us or to chastise us by engaging our imaginations and by leading us into creative struggle as we face our own questions of faith. In this way, the Bible can change our consciousness and transform our mythologies and world views.

The Wisdom Literature

From the wisdom literature emerges a vision of life and faith that is profoundly relational, the realization of which would create a world at peace.[15] At its center stands a mysterious and alluring woman. She is *hokmâh*, *sophia*, Lady Wisdom, or, as I prefer to call her, the Wisdom Woman. In all the texts in which she appears, her primary mode of being is affiliative. Her connections extend to all of reality. She is closely joined to the created world; she is God's intimate friend; she delights in the company of human beings. No aspect of reality is separated from her. She exists in it as if it were a tapestry of intertwined threads, patterned into a peaceful and harmonious unity with her at the center. Consequently, to follow the Wisdom Woman is to enter into this matrix of relationships, and, hence, to make a choice for peace rooted in justice.

In the Book of Proverbs (cc 1–9), this choice is depicted as concretely as possible. It is the choice of the young man between two women: one the seductress, the "Strange Woman," whose friendship leads to death; the other, the Wisdom Woman, whose intimacies bring blessing, life and relationships overflowing with joy. The personification of these points of view in feminine figures, at first glance, appears to offer women a niche of their own in the biblical traditions, otherwise so overwhelmingly masculine in language, imagery and experience. However that is not the case. This is no safe haven for women, at least, not without some critical cautions.

Both women, the Wisdom Woman and the Strange Woman, are male projections of opposing aspects of the human condition onto female figures. That is, these are not women as they were in Israelite society nor in other societies in the ancient world, nor are they women as we exist today, but stereotypes of femininity as men envisioned it. The Wisdom Woman and the Strange Woman are dialectical opposites. One is everything good, humanly desirable, and profitable for men. The other is everything harmful to men, the path to death, the speaker of lying words, the source of stolen pleasures. No woman, no human being, is that good or that bad.

However, just as the wisdom literature transcends the limitations of the patriarchal culture that produced it, so too the figure of the Wisdom Woman ultimately rises above narrow female stereotypes to take on a life of her own in the texts and in our imaginations. More than a potential marriage partner, she becomes a developed character in her own right, *ḥokmâh*, *sophia*, who calls all peoples into full human existence. And though scholars have been slow to recognize her true identity,[16] it seems clear that the Wisdom Woman is a divine being, an image of God herself.

Before all else the Wisdom Woman is a figure of poetry who appears in texts scattered throughout the wisdom corpus: Prv 1:20–33; 3:13–18; 4:4–9; 8:1–9:5; 31:10–29; Job 28; Sir 24; Wis 6:12–10:1; Bar 3:9–4:4. Her poetic nature requires that she be understood on many intertwined levels of meaning rather than in a flat or linear way. As a character of poetry she represents an insight into the nature of reality, designed to evoke emotional and intellectual responses from the reader. Poetry creates imaginative worlds to do precisely that. Its truth is determined by the degree to which its imaginative vision accurately represents reality.

Consequently, the Wisdom Woman cannot be reduced to a list of functions which she performs, though that can be given. She brings with her an aura, a haunting series of hints, allusions and revelations about the world and about God. Though the texts do not describe her in the specific biblical vocabulary of peace (*shālôm, eirēnē*), the life she brings overflows with peace in every dimension of the term, personal, social, cosmic. She is a metaphor leading us into the deepest mystery. In her the notion of *hokmâh* moves beyond a category to describe behavior and qualities of human beings to include a person who is herself Wisdom. She does not simply act in wise ways, nor is she merely a person who is said to be wise through and through, though she is that. She is Wisdom. She incarnates wisdom in all its aspects.

That the Wisdom Woman is no ordinary woman is clear from the traditions about her beginnings or, more accurately, her origins before the beginning of anything else. In a poem in Proverbs (8:22–31) Wisdom herself tells the story of her pre-existence.

> The Lord created me at the beginning of his work,
> the first of his acts of old.
> Ages ago I was set up,
> at the first, before the beginning of the earth (8:22–23).

The Hebrew verb, *qānâh*, here translated "created me," may be more accurately rendered "acquired me."[17] With this rendering God discovers rather than creates Wisdom. However, the point of these lines is the Wisdom Woman's pre-existence. Before the fashioning of the natural world which human beings take profoundly for granted, before things which seem to have existed forever, she existed. Before springs and mountains and hills, before dust and seas and the skies above, before the shaping of the sanctuary of the world which human beings were to inhabit, she was present (8:23–29).

Her transcendent origins establish her authority. In the ancient world the older the religious figures and traditions were believed to be, the more claim they had to reveal hidden truths. She is older than even the oldest thing we know, the earth itself. By placing her origins before the creation of the universe, the author makes the truth she speaks unquestionable.

However her pre-existence has a further function in this poem. It affirms her relationship with the world. Coming before it, she was both a witness to, and participant in, God's creative activity. "When he established the heavens, I was there" (8:27). "When he marked out the foundations of the earth, I was beside him" (8:30). She saw it all and she can testify to it. But she was more than a passive spectator of God's work. She was "like a master workman" (8:30), literally, an artisan. She participated in creation as the skilled craftswoman, the artist who forms, shapes and colors the world. The mysterious beauty and orderliness of the world sprang from her work.

The Wisdom Woman does not act alone. In this poem, she is not God but God's companion. "When he established the heavens, I was there. . . . When he marked out the foundations of the earth, there I was beside him." She was his co-worker, "daily his delight, rejoicing before him always" (8:30).

Proverbs 8 depicts a puzzling mutuality in her relationship with God. She is ever with him, joining in his work, imprinting it with her artistry, and living with God in shared delight. She is neither his subordinate nor his competitor. She is his partner, his co-artist and the focus of his joy. The poem intimates that the two are lovers joined in a world transcending the universe yet one with it. But Israel's God is one and that God has no consort, that God transcends sexuality. Such is Israel's insistence in face of the manipulative, sexual conceptions of the divine in the nations around it. There are not two gods in this poem. There is divine expression in male and female imagery, and, above all, in imagery of relationship.

The poem in Proverbs 8 has not yet reached its goal. Wisdom's existence before the creation of the world, her participation in that creation, and her relationship of love with its Creator are all prelude to her current preoccupation: the enjoyment of the inhabited world and delight in the children of humans (8:31). It is to this announcement that the poem has been pressing. Human beings and their habitat are her interests. Wisdom sets her gaze on them, and she takes pleasure in their humanity. Hence, those on whom this mysterious figure sets her loving gaze, that is, all people, are conferred with immense dignity.

The Wisdom Woman is the center of a matrix of relationships among God, the world and its human occupants. It is she who communicates among them; it is she who acts as the bridge between God, humans and the world. She reveals the world and God in their secrets and wonder to human beings. She is, then, the key to human enlightenment. The path to which she beckons is not for the isolated individual, competing for power or wealth. Her way is communal, collaborative, and inclusive. By following her, by uniting with her, her disciples enter into peaceful communion with all reality.

As in all true relationships, human relationship with the Wisdom Woman is reciprocal. She takes the initiative; humans respond with every possible effort. The Wisdom Woman appears suddenly, with no warning (Prv 1:20–32 and 8:1–6) in the streets, in the marketplace, on the top of the city walls, at the entrance of the city gates (1:20). These are all places where people come together to transact daily commerce and legal dealings in the ancient cities. In the thick of life at its shabbiest and its most exciting, in the routine of daily marketing and in the struggles of ordinary people to survive—it is there that the Wisdom Woman extends her invitation.

She delivers it in the style of a prophet, insistently, urgently: she "shouts with joy," she lifts up her voice, she calls, she speaks her words, trying to catch the attention of everyone in the town (see 8:1–3). Her audience is the simple, the foolish, the scorners (1:22; 8:5). Everyone is simple before Wisdom.[18]

> Her promises are startling.
> Look, I will pour out my spirit (*rûaḥî*) upon you.
> I will make my words known to you (Prv 1:23, my translation).

To maintain parallelism with the second line, *rûaḥî* is usually translated "my thoughts." However, the sense of the verse is better captured by the more literal Hebrew, "my spirit." To those who will accept her, Wisdom will reveal the fullness of her message, that is, herself. Relationship with her promises full mutuality. In this poem, however, the Wisdom Woman's self-donation is neither comforting nor encouraging. It is a sharp rebuke in the tradition of prophetic speech in which those who reject divine revelation are doomed.[19]

The purpose of Proverbs 1:20–33 is to emphasize the life and death choice facing Wisdom's audience. This poem draws an analogy between relationship with her and relationship with God. To refuse her and participation in her web of relationships is to condemn oneself to isolation and death.

Wisdom reiterates her invitation to life in peace and mutual harmony in Proverbs 9:1–5. In this narrative poem which brings to a climax the series of poems about her in chapters 8–9, she builds a house, perhaps symbolizing a temple or perhaps the world she helped to create. In that symbolic house she prepares a great festive banquet. She slaughters beasts, mixes wine and prepares the table. She sends out her maids to invite everyone who is simple to come to her banquet, to partake of her feast. Her table symbolizes life as it might be, a banquet table where all peoples participate in the delights of the meal, eating, drinking and enjoying full participation in the human community. These poetic images depict a world at peace, where interconnection rules, where competition and individ-ualism are banished and where the world and its riches are shared equally by all its peoples.

The significance of this invitation to the banquet of peace becomes apparent when one recognizes the full identity of the hostess. In the texts about the Wisdom Woman there are many indications, connotative rather than denotative, allusive rather than descriptive, that the Wisdom Woman is more than a cipher for the human virtue of wisdom. She is herself God. Much of what is said about her can only be said of God. She existed before the creation of the world and she participated in its formation as a major artisan (8:30). She is a tree of life and in her hand she holds life itself (Prv 3:16, 18). Through her, kings reign, princes rule, and rulers decree what is just (Prv 8:15). She pours out her spirit upon her followers and re-veals her words to the ones who seek her (Prv 1:23). These are activities of God. They are divine prerogatives, activities to benefit humankind which God alone performs.

In the impressionistic portraits of the Wisdom Woman, there are only hints of her divinity. Never does the Hebrew Scripture suggest that there are two gods, a male and female God, nor does it do any more than hint that Yahweh has a lover in the Wisdom Woman. In some of the poems about her, the Wisdom Woman seems to be a creature of Yahweh, though a privileged one, separate from God and delighting in the divine presence. But in other texts she represents another way to look at God, another metaphor to speak of the beauty, power and attraction that God holds out to human beings.

In Sirach 24, a poem in praise of Wisdom, written several centuries after Proverbs, the Wisdom Woman's origins are elaborated in a slightly different way than in Proverbs 8:22. In the Sirach poem she tells of coming forth from the mouth of the Most High; she is the Word of God (Sir 24:3). She is in-distinguishable from God's mind, God's will, God's love. As the Word of God, she "covered the earth like mist," she "dwelt in high places" and her "throne was a pillar of cloud."

Like a queen overseeing her domain, she wanders around the universe. "Alone I made the circuit of the vault of heaven and walked in the depths of the abyss. In the waves of the sea, in the whole earth, and in every people and nation I have gotten a possession" (Sir 24:3b–6). Though imaged differently than in Proverbs 8, the Sirach poem also portrays the Wisdom Woman, named *Sophia* in this Greek text, as the center of intertwining relationships. She traverses the whole of the cosmos, the realm of the earth as well as the heavenly sphere usually reserved for God. She is uniquely related to all the peoples and nations of the earth, as well as to the earth itself.

Then at God's command, the Word of God takes up special residence among the people of Israel, in the holy tabernacle of Jerusalem (vv. 8–12). There she flourishes and prospers (vv. 13–17), and there she again invites everyone to come and to eat and drink of her feast (vv. 19–22). That the Sirach poem is deliberately patterned after the poem in Proverbs 8 is quite clear. And though her roles are not the same here, she is again the thread that ties together all reality. However, in Sirach 24 there is a remarkable change in the language used to describe Wisdom's feast. What is to be eaten and drunk is *Sophia* herself.

> Those who eat me will hunger for more
> and those who drink me will thirst for more (Sir 24:21).

Anticipating eucharistic language of Christians, this poem implies that it is communion with her that brings all people into harmony and peace.

In a long passage in the Wisdom of Solomon (Wis 6:12–9:18), the last of the Old Testament wisdom books, claims for her divinity are extended even further. She is described as "radiant and unfading," "easily discerned by those who love her" (6:12) and "the fashioner of all things" (7:22).

> For in her there is a spirit that is intelligent, holy, unique, manifold, subtle, mobile, clear, unpolluted, distinct, invulnerable, loving the good, keen, irresistible, benefi-

cent, humane, steadfast, sure, free from anxiety, all-powerful, overseeing all and penetrating through all spirits that are intelligent and pure and most subtle. For wisdom is more mobile than any motion; because of her pureness she pervades and penetrates all things.

For she is a breath of the power of God and a pure emanation of the glory of the Almighty; therefore nothing defiled gains entrance into her. For she is a reflection of eternal light, and an image of his goodness (Wis 7:22–25).

To follow Wisdom, to embrace her and to live with her is, finally, to live with God. It is to recognize and to collaborate with the harmony, beauty and order of God in this world and to be transformed by it. To do so means to leave behind the illusion of isolation, that we each live alone, that our personal safety is all. To embrace Wisdom is to take a communal, holistic stance toward the world and its inhabitants, to live in communion with all that is, to live in peace.

The wisdom literature, therefore, presents a radical and liberative social vision. Like women's culture, wisdom literature insists on the centrality of relationship, on interconnection rather than independence, on reciprocity rather than competitive domination. Though biblical vocabulary of peace is absent from the texts considered, the passages about the Wisdom Woman create an imaginative world, a mythical vision, of a universe at peace. But this symbolic universe exists only in poetry. Our world is a place of domination, violence and death. Peace requires the mythology of wisdom where there is room for play and delight; where the earth, too, is treated with reverence; where life is cherished and where space is made for even the littlest and most insignificant to flourish.

The vision of Wisdom's banquet of peace does not end in the Old Testament. It was Elisabeth Schüssler Fiorenza[20] who observed the predominance of meals and festive banquets in the teaching and praxis of Jesus and their continuity with the wisdom tradition. Schüssler Fiorenza argues that this is no coincidence, nor even simply Jesus' appeal to a common human experience. The sharing of meals is a key revelatory aspect of Jesus's mission and of Jesus' God.

It is in Jesus' festive table sharing, not in the cultic meal, nor in the abstinence of the Baptist, who came "neither eating nor drinking," that the reign of God is disclosed. Proclaimed a glutton and a drunkard, Jesus' participation in meals with tax collectors and sinners, the outcast and the marginated, was a principal reason for his rejection by his own people and a shocking revelation of the ways of God.

Moreover, in the many parables about meals and banquets Jesus reveals "the inclusive graciousness and goodness" of God.[21] Jesus proclaims the God of all-inclusive love who accepts everyone and grants blessing and well-being to all. These are the characteristics of the Creator God, the *Sophia*-God of the wisdom traditions. Jesus' announcement of the rule of God in parables and images of the meal further elaborates the inclusive invitation he extends to his followers in the name of *Sophia*-God.

The royal banquet and the marriage feast symbolize the rule of God already present in Jesus and in his mission. The meal sharing of Christians, therefore, is a feast celebrating and actualizing the radical inclusiveness of *Sophia*-God of peace and communion rooted in justice. People of every kind are invited to the festive banquet table of God's rule. They come from the highways and the byways; they are the rejected, the unwashed and the insignificant. Those serving the table, the leaders of the community, lay no heavy burden on the guests, nor lord it over them. At this feast it is unnecessary for anyone to ask for a higher seat. All, from the least to the greatest, have equal honor at the table.

Jesus' vision is not exclusively an eschatological hope, a mythological promise. The reign of God is here now. Jesus' parables announced it and his praxis proclaimed it. They represent the way social relations should be conducted in the reign already begun—in mutuality, connectedness and community that excludes none and falsely exalts none.

If the question of the quality of relationship is at the heart of peace, then the evangelization of our patriarchal culture is an urgent task. Women's culture equips women and men for this work. The God of Wisdom, *Sophia* God, empowers women and men to bring everyone to the table of peace. The *Sophia* God cannot be the banner for war, nor the buttress of the rich, nor can she be invoked in the wasting of the earth. She releases her energy upon the simple to reconstitute the earth and to bring all peoples to the festive banquet of peace.

NOTES

. .

1 Robert J. Daly, et al., *Christian Biblical Ethics: From Biblical Reve-lation to Contemporary Christian Praxis: Method and Content* (New York: Paulist, 1984).
2 Beverly Wildung Harrison, "The Older Person's Worth in the Eyes of Society," in Carol S. Robb, ed., *Making the Connections: Essays in Feminist Social Ethics* (Boston: Beacon, 1985), p. 155.
3 For example, see Richard Slotkin, *Regeneration Through Violence: The Mythology of the American Frontier, 1600–1860* (Middletown: Wesleyan University, 1973).
4 See Daly, p. 126, for a discussion of the process by which a dom-inant mythology undergoes change in the face of new experience.
5 Anne Carr, "Theological Anthropology and the Experience of Women," *Chicago Studies* 19 (1980):113–128; Patricia Wilson Kast-ner, "Contemporary Feminism and the Christian Doctrine of the Human," *Word & World* 2 (1980):234–42; Jean Grimshaw, *Philos-ophy and Feminist Thinking* (Minneapolis: University of Minnesota, 1986); Gerda Lerner, *The Creation of Patriarchy* (Oxford: Oxford University, 1986).
6 Bell Hooks, *Feminist Theory: From Margin to Center* (Boston: South End Press, 1984), p. 126.
7 Lerner, p. 239; Astrid Albrecht-Heide, "The Peaceful Sex," in W. Chapkis, ed., *Loaded Questions: Women in the Military* (Amsterdam: Transnational Institute, 1981), pp. 83–87.
8 *Working* (New York: Avon, 1974), pp. 533–34.
9 Dorothy Soelle, *Union Seminary Quarterly Review* XXXVIII (1983):83–91.
10 Harrison, "The Power of Anger in the Work of Love," *Making the Connections*, p. 16. Lerner, p. 242, claims that women's culture "encompasses familial and friendship networks of women, their af-fective ties and rituals." Women's culture is not a subculture be-cause it represents the social relations of half of humanity. Women, therefore, live in two cultures, the dominant culture and their own culture.

[11] "Family Structure and Feminine Personality," in Michelle Zimbalist Rosaldo and Louise Lamphere, eds., *Woman Culture and Society* (Stanford: Stanford University, 1974), pp. 17–42.

[12] Carol Gilligan, *In a Different Voice: Psychological Theory and Women's Development* (Cambridge: Harvard University, 1982). See also the criticisms of her work and her reply, "On *In a Different Voice:* An Interdisciplinary Forum," *Signs: Journal of Women in Culture and Society* 11 (1986):304–333.

[13] Grimshaw, pp. 190–94.

[14] Paulo Freire, *Pedagogy of the Oppressed* (New York: Herder and Herder, 1971); Elizabeth Janeway, *Powers of the Weak* (New York: Morrow Quill, 1981).

[15] These points are developed further in my book, *The Wisdom Literature,* The Message of Biblical Spirituality 5 (Wilmington: Michael Glazier, 1988).

[16] Gerhard von Rad (*Wisdom in Israel* [Nashville: Abingdon, 1972], pp. 71–72) believes that Wisdom is a personification of the order in the universe; R. B. Y. Scott (*Proverbs. Ecclesiastes,* Anchor Bible, vol. 18 [Garden City: Doubleday, 1965], pp. 70–72) maintains that Wisdom is not God but an attribute of God; Samuel Terrien (*The Illusive Presence: Toward a New Biblical Theology,* Religious Perspectives 26 [San Francisco: Harper & Row, 1978], p. 357) calls her "the mediatrix of presence."

[17] Bruce Vawter, "Prov 8:22: Wisdom and Creation," in *The Path of Wisdom: Biblical Investigation,* Background Books 3 (Wilmington: Michael Glazier, 1986), pp. 161–77.

[18] Phyllis Trible, "Wisdom Builds a Poem: The Architecture of Proverbs 1:20–33," *Journal of Biblical Literature* 94 (1975):512.

[19] Roland E. Murphy ("Wisdom and Creation," *Journal of Biblical Literature* 104 [1985]:9) speaks of her invitation as "the voice of the Lord." See the important work of Claudia Camp, *Wisdom and the Feminine in the Book of Proverbs,* Duke University Dissertation, 44 (1983), p. 196-A.

[20] *In Memory of Her: A Feminist Theological Reconstruction of Christian Origins* (New York: Crossroad, 1983), pp. 118–120 and 130–140.

[21] Ibid., p. 119.

Chapter Three

MATTHEW 5:9: "BLESSED ARE THE PEACEMAKERS, FOR THEY SHALL BE CALLED SONS OF GOD"*

. . . . . .

Hugh M. Humphrey

Although Mt 5:9 has been called the "Magna Carta" of the peace movement by the present Pontiff,[1] it would seem that peacemaking among nations was not its original implication.[2] This intuitive premise comes from two considerations. First, the "universal" sense of "peace" seems to have been considered and explicitly rejected in Mt 10:34 where Matthew has modified a Q saying (Lk 12:51) into an emphatic declaration: "I have not come to bring peace" on earth. Secondly, there is the consideration of the larger social world of the evangelist. An era of social and civil peace existed throughout the Roman Empire during the first century.[3] Admittedly there were local, temporary disruptions, but the prevailing perception among the citizens of the Empire would have been of stability and, at least as an empire, of security. How would Matthew have made sense of "peace-making" as an activity among nations when no rival government was seriously competing with the Roman Empire and everyone knew this? If Matthew intended the beatitude to carry a "universal" sense,

---

*Vocabulary in this chapter makes frequent reference to masculine terms, such as "sons of God." This is not intended as sexist language. The words are used as direct

at least some of his audience/community were Gentiles and would have surely thought it a frivolous statement, since peace in that sense existed already and did not have to be "made."

If this intuition is accurate, then it makes explicit a hermeneutical process to which Christians do not frequently advert, namely, that there is a dialectic going on between the world view of the writer and the world view of the reader. The dialectic is that of peacemaking as an activity of Christians *within* their community in distinction from peacemaking as activity of Christians *outside* their community in the world at large. These activities would provide mutual challenge. Contemporary Christians who begin with the presuppositions of a community opened to the world would be challenged by the presuppositions of the biblical author that peace is a task within the community of believers. On the other hand, the presuppositions of the present day would lead believers to read the peace mandate in a way that is faithful to the biblical mandate but within a new world of meaning. In what follows we will seek to verify our intuition about the presupposed world view of the author of Matthew and thus point to the implicit hermeneutical methodology that must underlie present-day reading of the text.

It would seem that neither the larger context of Mt 5:9 (the Sermon on the Mount) nor its immediate context (the beatitudes) provides a definite basis of interpretation for the meaning of the peace-making beatitude. A consideration of Matthew's extension of Mk 9:50, however, and of the challenge to be "salt" (5:13) and "light" (5:14) before the world (5:16) suggests that it is in its *intra* community peace-making that Matthew saw his community showing itself to be righteous "sons of God" (5:9).

---

quotations from Matthew or to make clear reference to specific texts of Matthew. Such use is necessary for clear exegetical analysis and comparisons of texts. The thought of Matthew should, of course, be interpreted to include all persons, both male and female.

The Context of Matthew 5:9

The beatitudes in Mt 5:3–10 are *not* really a completely independent passage which can be dealt with apart from the rest of the Sermon on the Mount in Matthew 5–7. If Mt 5:21–46 and 6:1–7:20 describe the good works which the "wise man"/disciple must do to enter into the kingdom of heaven, the beatitudes describe the kind of person who does them. While "righteousness" is the general designation for a way of life that requires distinctive, specific actions (cf. Mt 6:1 in relation to 6:2–7:2), the beatitudes describe a single, fundamental attitude ("for righteousness' sake," 5:10) under its various aspects. Thus, any one characteristic would include the others (and Mt 5:9 could not be interpreted in dissonance with others).

It would, of course, make the interpretation of some passages of the Sermon on the Mount, including Mt 5:9, a great deal simpler if there were a consistent perspective throughout these chapters. Unfortunately there are at least three groups in focus and some specific references are unclear for that reason.

Clearly there is the group of those beyond the Christian community, the *complete outsiders:*

Gentiles (5:47; 6:32)
Tax Collectors (5:46)
Scribes and Pharisees (5:20)
Thieves (6:19–20)

Just as clearly there is the group of those Christians who are admirable for their righteousness, for their effort to practice Jesus' way, the *complete insiders:*

The wise man who hears Jesus' words and does them (7:24)
The Christian who acknowledges Jesus as Lord and does the will of the Father (7:21)

Those who are like sound trees, bearing good fruit
(7:17)
Those who enter by the narrow gate and find "life"
(7:14)
The "men of little faith" (6:30)
Your brethren (5:47)
Your brother (6:3–5; 5:23–24)
You (5:13–16)
The blessed (5:3–10, 11–12)

Another dialectic, however, is *also* present in the tension between the admirable insiders and the less rigorous, more com-
placent pursuers of the way of righteousness. That this group
is in focus is clear from the development in Mt 7:15–27: there
are "false prophets" (7:15) who are like "bad trees," bearing
"evil fruit" (7:17); at the judgment (7:22), these "evildoers"
(7:23) will *not* "enter the kingdom of heaven" (7:21) *"even
though they acknowledge Jesus as Lord "* (7:21–22); these persons
who hear the words of Jesus, but do not do them will be like foolish
men (7:26).

Because this second dialectic exists, some other references to persons or groups in the Sermon on the Mount become ambiguous. The hypocrites of Mt 6:2, 5 and 16, for
example, could be non-Christians, or "outsiders"; *but* one
must consider the possibility also that the "hypocrites" are
themselves members of the Christian community who either
want others to admire them for laudable reasons (cf. Mt 5:16),
in which case the "men" would be outsiders, or want praise
and adulation, in which case the "men" could in turn be either
"insiders" or "outsiders."[4]

Mt 5:9, therefore, is part of an overall development in
which there is enough ambiguity in the direction of Matthew's
dialectic in the Sermon on the Mount not to be able to determine simply and precisely with whom "the peacemakers"
make peace: those beyond the Christian community (individ-

uals or groups) or those within the Christian community (the "brother who has something against you" in 5:23, the "brother" whom you judge to be flawed in some way in 7:1–5, the "false prophets . . . in sheep's clothing" in 7:15).

Yet there is also no clear direction of interpretation for Mt 5:9 from the immediate context of the beatitudes. Robert Guelich argues[5] that the "non-parallel" beatitudes (Mt 5:5, 7–9) were also, for the most part, pre-Matthean and in Q.[6] Guelich is impressed by the relationship between these and other Q materials[7] and by the fact that Mt 5:7–9 "form an ascending scale in their promises and consequently in their order."[8] Matthew's own redactional activity, for Guelich, was in the direction of further "aligning the traditional beatitudes with Is 61:1–3"[9] and in the construction of 5:10.

> This work has resulted in two groups of four Beatitudes (5:3–6; 5:7–10). The first, beginning with an allusion to Is 61:1–3 (cf. 5:3), and the second, concluding with the same allusion (cf. 5:10), form an *inclusio*. Furthermore, the first Beatitude of each group concludes with a reference to righteousness [*dikaiosynè*] (5:6, 10).[10]

Although Neil McEleney's reconstruction of the process by which the Matthean beatitudes came to their present form differs slightly from Guelich's,[11] he does advance an interpretation of Mt 5:9 as part of a three-beatitude set (Mt 5:7–9) introduced by the evangelist:

> These beatitudes set a high standard, requiring interior dispositions of forgiveness and mercy (Mt 5:7), purity of intention (Mt 5:8), and a genuine effort to promote peaceful living within the community (Mt 5:9).[12]

This expansion of the list of beatitudes was made to prepare for other materials in Matthew 5–7: "The peacemakers are to act with god-like impartiality towards all and to reconcile differences so as to be children of God (see Mt 5:43–48)."[13]

Rudolf Schnackenburg attempts to make that connection

between Mt 5:9 and 5:44–45a more precise[14] because Mt 5:9–10 conform well with 5:44–45a: (1) there is the coincidence of "sons of God" in 5:9 and "sons of your Father" in 5:45a; (2) the beatitude addressed to "the persecuted" in 5:10 corresponds to "pray for those who persecute you" in 5:44; and (3) since Mt 5:45a, "so that you may be sons of your father in heaven," can be interpreted as an eschatological gift of God, an eschatological perspective in Mt 5:44–45 would be yet another parallel between 5:9–10 and 5:44–45. Matthew would, accordingly, have *at least* had the "love of your enemies" material in mind when he composed 5:10 and *probably* allowed that material to influence *both* beatitudes in 5:9 and 5:10 when he reworked the entire second strophe (vv. 7–10). Thus, the peacemaker is continually called to overcome any kind of hatred or hostility, even in the context of persecution.[15]

Schnackenburg then examines the wider context of the first gospel. The materials in Mt 5:21–24, 7:3 and 5:47 are concerned with how to treat one's "brother" in the Christian community and this perspective is further developed in terms of Matthew's treatment in Mt 18:15–35. Thus Schnackenburg concludes with the judgment that the Matthean context generally does not support a univocal interpretation for Mt 5:9 and "peacemaking." On the one hand one must recognize that the gospel speaks of hostility and persecution coming from outside the community; on the other hand, the internal tensions and controversies which exist in the community and which threaten the brotherhood and sisterhood can only be excluded from view with difficulty. It is probable, therefore, that the formulation of the peacemaking beatitude was intentionally broadly defined.[16]

The Schnackenburg view, therefore, would give peacemaking a reference beyond the community (in contrast to the interpretation suggested by McEleney): the Christian community and its individual members will be "blessed" as "sons of God" at the eschatological judgment if they direct that undifferentiated love (cf. Mt 5:45–47) which must surely be present among them (cf. chap. 18) toward their enemies/persecutors/outsiders.

Schnackenburg, however, does not present a satisfactory explanation for *why* Matthew would have composed the "second strophe" (Mt 5:7–10). He seems to say that because Matthew composed 5:10 and because 5:9–10 would be parallel with Mt 5:44–45, Matthew saw a close connection between Mt 5:9 and 10.[17] What is omitted is a reason for Matthew's also including Mt 5:7–8. Or for the ascending order of rewards in 5:7–9. Or for Matthew's not having simply stayed closer to the (presumable) order of Q as now evidenced in Lk 6:20–23, 27. Indeed, the placement of so much material between Mt 5:9–10 and 5:44–45 would seem to work against Schnackenburg's suggestion; the materials of Mt 5:44–45 (Lk 6:27–28, 35) were in much closer alignment with Mt 5:11–12 (Lk 6:22–23) already in Q; why separate them more if they were meant to interpret each other, and in turn to interpret Mt 5:9?

The immediate context of the beatitudes nonetheless offers several considerations for the interpretation of Mt 5:9. The Matthean construction of 5:10 has created a unity for the beatitudes of 5:3–10 by means of an inclusion and organized them into two strophes, the last verse of which in each case names "righteousness" as the causative factor. If the first strophe blesses the internal dispositions of the righteous follower of Jesus, the second appears to bless the activity of the righteous Christian towards others (Christians, as McEleney suggests?). Since nothing in Mt 5:7–10 itself identifies those with whom one must "make peace," that remains unclear. Still, peacemaking is an activity that is of primary importance because of the blessing attached to it; it is an activity characteristic of the Christian because of the "kingdom of heaven" references in 5:3 and 5:10 and the content of the salt and light sayings in 5:13–16; and it is associated with, inspired by, or an aspect of the "righteousness" (5:6, 10) which is to characterize the Christian's inner disposition and outward activity.

Peacemaking in Matthew

Mt 5:9 is the only instance of *eirēnopoios* (peacemaker) in the New Testament. What is equally striking is that the root term "peace" (the making of which merits a beatitude!) occurs only four times in Matthew, all of them in chapter 10; there the term describes a quality possessed by the members of the Christian community; indeed such is the conception in Mt 10:13; the Christian missionary is instructed: "As you enter the house, salute it (v. 12). And if the house is worthy, let *your* peace come upon it; but if it is not worthy, let *your* peace return to you."

Matthew's gospel, however, reflects a double sense of "peace."[18] Matthew's references to peace in 10:13 refer to that quality which the members of the Christian community possess and which they may offer to others who would join their community. What Matthew chooses to emphasize, however, is *not* peace as a *gift* to be enjoyed (i.e. as in Mt 10:13), *but* peace as *a responsibility*, of individual Christians, in a community or brotherhood/sisterhood setting.

The manner in which Mt 18:1–35 modifies the materials of Mk 9:33–50 is the evidence for this judgment because, while Matthew will omit Mark's reference to being "at peace with one another" (Mk 9:50), he presents in its place an elaborate composition of sayings of Jesus on just how fellow members of the Christian community are to act toward one another. Mt 18:15–35 is a description of that effort of "peacemaking" which is the responsibility of Christians.

The coherence of the plan of Matthew 18 was achieved by means of the modification and expansion of the materials in Mk 9:33–50. The first part of this discourse, Mt 18:1–14, is largely taken from Mk 9:33–48. The second part, Mt 18:15–35, does not ostensibly use any Markan material. *Yet it has been prepared for by Matthew's treatment of Mk 9:37, 38–41 in Mt 18:5[19] and it takes its place in the narrative line precisely at the point where Mk 9:50 had spoken about "being at peace with one another."* Mt

18:15–35, therefore, seems to have been intended as a development of or commentary upon that phrase. That this "peacemaking" enterprise within the community and among the disciples was very important to Matthew is clear from the extent of the development in 18:15–35, the emphasizing of this willingness to forgive "your brother" as the Father's will (18:35) and by the repositioning of Mk 9:49–50 in a place of prominence at the beginning of the Sermon on the Mount (Mt 5:9, 13).[20]

In emphasizing the effort Christians should make to "be at peace with one another," Matthew does not, it is true, use the words of Mk 9:50, but *describes* the effort which must be made to remove discord and division among members of the Matthean community.

Thus, the materials reviewed above suggest a consistent background and focus of meaning for Mt 5:9: "Peacemaking" is the effort to break down strife between individuals within the Christian community;[21] it is the readiness to respect other Christians as being "in Christ" because they believe in him and to forgive without limit the other brother's sins against you if he or she repents. To come to agreement in this fashion is to make Christ himself present (Mt 18:19–20) in the community and to establish anew its fundamental unity. In this way, the disciples show themselves to be unique, like "salt" (Mt 5:13). The "peacemaking" which is blessed in Mt 5:9 seems, therefore, not to be directed toward nations but toward other Christians; it is not universalistic in Matthew's mind, but ecclesiological, a responsibility of Christians toward Christians.

Matthew's Community: Threatened by Internal Discord and Called to Be Sons of God

If Mt 5:9 should be interpreted in terms of urging peacemaking among the individual members of the Matthean church, one would expect, from the emphasis given to this beatitude (i.e. its being given the status of a beatitude and then placed at the end of the ascending scale in Mt 5:7–9), that the gospel of Matthew would to some extent reflect a situation needing such intra-community, peace-making initiatives. The works of J. Kingsbury,[22] W. Thompson,[23] and J. Meier[24] describe a community threatened by internal discord, badly needing to hear and to heed an assertion of the inseparability of forgiving one's brother, of peacemaking and love of neighbor which should characterize the followers of Christ.

In Kingsbury's judgment, the Reason for Speaking in Parables (Mt 13:10–17) and the Interpretation of the Parable of the Sower (Mt 13:18–23) are "directed exclusively to the disciples, or Church."[25] Thus the various kinds of response referred to in the Interpretation of the Parable of the Sower are those of Christians (all four groups have "heard the word of the kingdom") of varying degrees of commitment to the righteousness required by Jesus' commandment of love. Even the "affliction or persecution" which causes the seed sown on rocky ground to fall away (cf. Mt 13:18–23!) is given a general sense to denote all manner of distress which may be directed at the individual by "even other apostate Christians because of his allegiance to Jesus, his Lord."[26]

W. Thompson analyzed Mt 17:22–18:35 and concluded that "the central instruction (18:1–20) reveals a divided community."[27] The situation implied by these instructions was one of internal dissension; its dimensions are echoed in the predictions of the eschatological discourse (Mt 24:10–13) and evidently were the experiential basis for Matthew's redactional work in chapter 18.[28]

J. Meier's description of the Matthean church sees profound difficulties confronting it: "major changes, all occurring in a relatively short time-span, created a crisis of identity" and "closely tied to this crisis was the crisis of authority within the church."[29] An examination of Mt 23:5; 23:6, and 23:7–10 suggested to Meier that Matthew is countering a kind of "nascent 'clericalism.' "

> Matthew may see in all these tendencies the danger that
> a good and necessary leadership role will turn into domi-
> nation, monopoly, and "clericalism." It is against such ex-
> cesses and trappings arising among the official teachers in
> the church, and not against church leadership and teach-
> ing in itself, that Matthew directs his attack in 23:1–12.[30]

These three descriptions, therefore, began from different
starting points, yet their judgment coincides: there is evidence
in Matthew's gospel that all is not well in the Matthean church;
not all are "salt" and "light" to the world and so there is a need
to challenge the Matthean Christians to *be* "salt" and "light"
and "perfect" (5:48), to "show yourselves to be sons of your
Father" (5:45).[31] The divisions of various kinds portrayed in
Paul's correspondence to Corinth seem to have had their par-
allels in the Matthean church: the attraction of the less ethi-
cally rigorous social world beyond the Matthean church and
the harassment to conform to prevailing social mores seem to
have led some members to be less enthusiastic pursuers of
righteousness than others; heeding "false prophets" led to
theological and ethical disagreements; some members of the
community were led to drop out because of scandalous (to
them) behavior by other Christians and they were in turn "des-
pised" for that scrupulosity (Mt 18:10–14). Indeed, some individuals so flagrantly and deliberately abused the common
understanding of how members of Matthew's church should
conduct themselves that the community had to adopt a pro-
cedure to safeguard its ethical "purity," even if that entailed
the excommunication of the unrepentant member (Mt 18:15–
17). Still, however irritating and however frequent the injury
suffered at the hands of another member of the Matthean
church, he or she must be forgiven if he or she does repent:
more important than the rights of the aggrieved individual
Christian is the unity of the whole church, in which Christ
himself is present (18:19–20). Every effort made to let unity
prevail is an effort made to sustain that "peace" which is the
precious possession of the Christian individually and as a mem-

ber of his or her community. And, when there is peace and
unity within the community, it witnesses to the world that it
is the community of the righteous, of "the sons of God."[32]

Conclusion

The purpose of this study has been to recover the meaning the evangelist would have intended when he wrote
"blessed are the peacemakers for they shall be called sons of
God." Since the interpretation which seems required by the
language of the beatitude itself and a consideration of the *Sitz-
im-Leben* of the Matthean community as well as by the ideological, non-conciliatory attitude of the evangelist is in terms
of accomplishing peace and unity *within* the Matthean community, a further question must be pursued. How can Mt 5:9
be legitimately used to sustain those efforts at conciliation and
peaceful coexistence which many Christians today feel
obliged—as Christians!—to pursue? How can a meaning for
the beatitude in Mt 5:9 be based upon that beatitude when it
so exceeds the meaning intended for it by the evangelist (*and
his church!*)?

We need, therefore, to define the hermeneutic which,
while avoiding both fundamentalism and eisegetical interpretations (i.e., reading into a text what is not there), will provide
a legitimate continuity between our present-day understanding of the Christian experience and the language of the New
Testament we use to inspire and encourage it. We need, I
think, to become the scribe who can bring out of his treasure
what is new and what is old (Mt 13:52).

Matthew's Gospel provides some indications of the direction which that evangelist-author would have taken in today's
discussion. On the one hand, Matthew's community was concerned for the world and its members were urged by the evangelist to be a "light" to the world around them (5:16); indeed,
there was even an outreach to it (10:28). But there was also a

sense that what it possessed was *qualitatively* different, a vital participation in a reality that was "eschatological" or *God*-given and not human-achieved. The "peace" which it enjoyed was an "eschatological blessing" and as such was just different in kind from the "peace" which human beings accomplish through good will and negotiation and compromise. The community could offer its peace to the world around them (10:12) but if that world was not yet ready to discern the eschatological blessing it presented, then the community could not continue its witness to that kind of peace which it knows from its community experience to be beyond the reach of human effort. And, fundamentally, that eschatological peace was inseparable from the experience of the presence of Jesus within the community of those who gather in his name (18:20).

Matthew's gospel states the challenge: Christians *must* "make peace" *among themselves* so that they become an example to the world of a people enjoying the eschatological blessings, attract others and teach others that the *content* of the life they experience is qualitatively different. Matthew would remind us that the challenge cannot be ignored: there is a danger in not responding to the task of *being* "salt" (5:13) and "light" (5:14): not all who call Jesus "Lord" will enter into the kingdom (7:21). Blessed, indeed, are then those who "make peace" and work toward unity among the brethren who confess Jesus; they become to the world at large a sign of the presence of Jesus among them and shall be called "sons of God."

NOTES

. .

1. John Paul II suggested a universal sense when he spoke March 6, 1983 at an open-air Mass in El Salvador.
2. This study would best be understood as preliminary to the effort of developing a hermeneutic in which one can move from the understanding of the Christian experience which found expression in the New Testament texts to the understanding which motivates the Christian's broad concern today for social issues such as peace and justice for all men.
3. Helmut Koester, *History, Culture, and Religion of the Hellenistic Age,* vol. 1 of *Introduction to the New Testament* (Philadelphia/Berlin and New York: Fortress/De Gruyter, 1982), pp. 307–17; that peace perdured is observed on pp. 307, 308, 317. Cf. also Eduard Lohse, *The New Testament Environment* (Nashville: Abingdon, 1976), pp. 201–7.
4. The references to "men" in Mt 6:1, 2, 5, 16 are similarly ambiguous. The usage of "men" in Mt 5:19, implying that they are members of the kingdom of heaven, suggests an "insider" reference there; and the parallel between Mt 6:14–15 and 18:35 suggests an "insider" reference is intended there also. Yet "men" in Mt 5:16, it would seem, could be argued either way. Finally, in view of the presence of the second dialectic mentioned above, is it really clear who "your neighbor" (5:43), "your enemies (5:44), "those who persecute you" (5:44) and the "unjust" (5:45) are? These terms all occur in a passage (5:43–48) which could be read plausibly in terms of *either* dialectic!
5. Robert A. Guelich, "The Matthean Beatitudes: 'Entrance-Requirements' or Eschatological Blessings," *Journal of Biblical Literature* 95 (1976): 415–34.
6. Cf. ibid., p. 426.
7. Ibid., pp. 421–22.
8. Ibid., pp. 422–23.
9. Ibid., p. 431; cf. pp. 427–31.
10. Ibid., p. 432.

¹¹ Neil J. McEleney, "The Beatitudes of the Sermon on the Mount/ Plain," *Catholic Biblical Quarterly* 43 (1981):1–13. While Guelich distinguishes between pre-Matthean Q as the source for Mt 5:5, 7–9 and the redactional work of the evangelist Matthew, McEleney attributes Mt 5:7–9, 10 to the evangelist Matthew and Mt 5:5 to "the Matthean Redactor" (?).

¹² Ibid., p. 10.

¹³ Ibid.

¹⁴ Rudolf Schnackenburg, "Die Seligpreisung der Friedensstifter (Mt 5, 9) in mattäischen Kontext," *Biblische Zeitschrift* 26 (1982):161–78. The article does not refer to McEleney's work.

¹⁵ Ibid., p. 169.

¹⁶ Ibid., p. 174.

¹⁷ Schnackenburg leaves open the pre-Matthean or redactional origin of Mt 5:9 (see ibid., pp. 166–67).

¹⁸ A similar twofold sense for the term "peace" occurs in Rom 14:17–19; Eph 4:1–3; and Jas 3:17–18. These texts suggest that "peace" was a term which *described both the uniqueness of the Christian community* in its love and practical concern for each of the brothers and sisters within it *and also the responsibility of the individual Christians* toward each other. It would seem that Mk 9:50b, "Have salt in yourselves, and be at peace with one another," ties these two aspects together.

¹⁹ Matthew retains the first part of Mk 9:37 but omits the second part as well as 9:38–41 (at least in this context). The effect is to conjoin the two general statements of Mk 9:37a and 9:42 in Mt 18:5–6 (note the *d'/* in Mt 18:6), making them serve as headings for the two discussions which follow in inverse order. That is, Mt 18:5, "Whoever receives one such child in my name, receives me," indicates the general motive underlying the *intracommunity* relationships discussed in 18:15–35. And 18:6 announces the concern of the immediately following material in Mt 18:7–14.

²⁰ The words about the uniqueness of the disciples as "salt" have been moved to the Sermon on the Mount, Mt 5:13 (where they have been extended by the "light" metaphor), in close proximity to the beatitude on peacemaking, Mt 5:9. Thus Mk 9:50b, "have salt in yourselves, and be at peace with one another," appears in inverted order in Mt 5:9, 13.

²¹ A similar emphasis on the community context for peacemaking in

Matthew's view is asserted by Henry Wansbrough in "Blessed are the Peacemakers" (*The Way* 22 [1982]:10–17). He also notes that if Mt 5:21–26 and 5:43–48 (the first and last parts of 5:21–43) are the negative and positive formulations of the love commandment, the "first correction presupposes a state of fairly extreme hostility within the community" (ibid., p. 15).

22 Jack Dean Kingsbury, *The Parables of Jesus in Matthew 13: A Study in Redaction-Criticism* (Richmond: John Knox Press, 1969).

23 William G. Thompson, *Matthew's Advice to a Divided Community: Mt. 17, 22–18, 35*, Analecta Biblica vol. 44 (Rome: Biblical Institute, 1970).

24 Raymond E. Brown, S.S. and John P. Meier, *Antioch and Rome: New Testament Cradles of Catholic Christianity* (New York: Paulist Press, 1983), cf. pp. 57–72.

25 Kingsbury, p. 63.

26 Ibid., p. 59.

27 Thompson, p. 259.

28 Ibid., p. 263.

29 Brown, p. 58.

30 Ibid., p. 71.

31 Mt 5:44 asserts that the Christians are to love their enemies and pray for those who persecute them "so that you may be sons of your Father who is in heaven" (5:45). Is the becoming "sons" a present condition or an eschatological blessing? If the verb *genesthe* is an ingressive aorist, it denotes not the beginning point, but a *gradual* becoming. In this case Matthew's form of the saying means:

> Love your enemies
>   and pray for those who persecute you,
> so that you may *show yourselves to be*
>   sons of your Father who is in heaven.

This interpretation would then be consistent with the sense of "sons of God" in Gal 3:26 and Rom 8:14 as a reference to the present, righteous people, unified by their having the Spirit (of Christ) in them (cf. Mt 28:20) and by their being already righteous in their actions.

[32] In addition to Mt 5:44–45 (n. 31), cf. Gal 3:26 and Rom 8:14 in their contexts. For further materials, see Brendan Byrne, *'Sons of God'—'Seed of Abraham': A Study of the Idea of the Sonship of God of All Christians in Paul Against the Jewish Background,* Analecta Biblica, Vol. 83 (Rome: Biblical Institute, 1979).

Chapter Four

PEACE AND PRAISE IN LUKE

. . . . . .

David P. Reid, SS.CC.

This presentation is an exercise in biblical theology, which is conscious of both method and content. Its starting point is Luke's preferred world view which is a picture of the Christian movement as a community of praise. The text would have the sensitive reader as also a member of this community. Thus author and reader enjoy a shared world view. Given the complementarity of these particular starting points, Luke's presentation of a community of praise provides insights into how life in a community of praise may be a way to peace in our world today.

Calling Forth a Community of Praise

Luke invites his reader to give glory and praise to God. The gospel begins with Zechariah praising God in the temple (1:18) and ends with the newly born Christian community in Jerusalem joyfully speaking the praises of God (24:53). Luke makes the reader part of the community of praise. The continuity between the new and the old is a concern for all New Testament writers; so it is a concern for Luke. He establishes that continuity in the praise of God: the community who praised God in times past, in the ministry of Jesus, in response to the proclamation of the good news. Modern biblical scholars discuss the stages in Luke's presentation of salvation history.[1] The thread linking all these stages, carrying the purposes of God right into the present, is Luke's insight that God is at all

times establishing a community of divine praise and glory.
This presents a starting point in our study of Luke.

Luke evokes this purpose of God in the angelic salutation.

> Glory to God in high heaven
> peace on earth to those on whom his favor rests (2:14).[2]

The choice of words in Lk 2:14 presents a variety of settings
in which one hears the proclamation of Jesus' birth. Stuhlmueller notes, for example, "that the song of the angels gives
a liturgical setting to the birth of Jesus as well as an eschatological aura (19:38).''[3] The chiastic structure of the verse
(glory/peace; heaven/earth; God/those on whom God's favor
rests) suggests a setting of creation. In this setting, the salutation benefits from the Old Testament insight that the earth
was made for humankind. An unpeopled earth would be in-
conceivable.[4] This understanding receives beautiful expression in Is 45:18.

> For thus says the Lord,
> The creator of the heavens, who is God,
> the designer and maker of the earth who established it,
> not creating it to be a waste,
> but designing it to be lived in (NAB).

This vertical dimension of creation interacts with the horizon-
tal dimension of history, the life of humankind on earth: not
just humankind in general but humankind specified as recipient of God's election and mercy.

God establishes peace on earth in and through the people
for whom God created the earth. Peace on earth is the working
out of God's glory. This suggests history, the arena for all human striving for peace, as the focus of God's activity as Creator. Irenaeus would be pleased to have his famous dictum
paraphrased: the glory of God is a human being fully alive and
engaged in peacemaking.

Luke offers in the angelic salutation a missionary profile for his two-volume work. The birth of Jesus is set within the Empire (2:1; 3:1).[5] Is Luke comparing the *pax Romana* and the peace of Christ or is he coopting the former for the good of the Christian mission?[6] However this question is decided, the peace of Christ is an offer and a challenge. The salutation is not merely a declaration of present peace but it is also an expression of eschatological hope. The words of the angelic choir ("Glory to God, etc.") are no excuse for complacency but a summons to a new integration of the human and the divine as the agenda of a redeemed humankind.

Within the literary world which Luke creates in his writing, the word "favor" (*eudokia*) carries earth-bound and social understandings. In Lk 4:19 such an understanding is present: ". . . and to announce a year of favor to the Lord." There, a different Greek word is found (*dektos*) but the same Hebrew idea of favor is present. Peace is no longer a private, individual pursuit, but it is a public, community-building proclamation of the reign of God. And peace had always been the concern of kings.

In ancient royal ideology, the king was responsible for peace and praise: the peace of humankind by looking to the welfare of his subjects, the praise of God by building and maintaining a temple. With regard to peace, Psalm 72 functions as a job description of the king in Israel. P. E. Bonnard studied this psalm apropos of Luke.[7] He is very careful not to make any claims for direct influence of Psalm 72 on Luke. However, both the author of the psalm and Luke have common themes, principally the king's care of the poor. The prayer, with which the psalm opens, asks that the king be endowed with justice, that he might judge rightly for the poor who are God's people:

> O God, with your judgment endow the king,
> and with your justice the king's son;
> He shall govern your people with justice
> and your afflicted ones with judgment (Ps 72:1–2 NAB).

Justice for the poor is coupled with peace.

> The mountains shall yield peace for the people
> and the hills justice.
> He shall defend the afflicted among the people,
> save the children of the poor
> and crush the oppressor (vv. 3–4).

As Bonnard notes, the psalm is not referred to any one king; it may have been constantly reread in light of the people's expectations, even of a foreigner who may one day come as king. Ultimately, the description, going beyond all common standards of royal leadership, fits only the action of God through mediation of a human. The psalm fits Jesus the Messiah in a special way. In Jesus, as unique savior, there is established peace for God's people and for all nations.[8] Bonnard does not refer to Lk 2:14 but his study warrants our acceptance of Psalm 72 as indicative of Luke's religious background.

As mentioned, the king is equally concerned with the praise and the glory of God. The king is concerned with the temple. When God is hailed as king, he is honored as the one who established the abode of his presence. Take, for example, Psalm 29. This is an enthronement psalm, which W. Brueggemann describes as a "concrete enactment of kingship."[9]

The psalm which begins: "Give to the Lord glory and praise" (v. 1) concludes: "may the Lord bless his people with peace" (v. 11). Between this invocation and conclusion, the psalm describes a stormy theophany of the voice of God with explicit reference to the enthronement of the Lord above the flood forever. The voice of the Lord is the word of God spoken to Israel in its long historical journey with God. The themes of peace and praise are given a new vibrancy as the community gathers to praise this wonderful God of creation and history. "And in his temple all say, 'glory' " (v. 9). God is praised in the calling forth of a community of praise who respond to God's word spoken the length and breadth of the land. The twinning of praise and peace in Psalm 29 presents a background for appreciating them in Luke, whose lasting concern is to call forth a community of praise and peace.

A Samaritan Admitted to the Community of Praise

The story of the Grateful Samaritan serves as our guide in this section of the essay. It illustrates how the biblical text sometimes makes its ethical points through narrative. The story is unique to the third gospel, 17:11–19, although probably not of Lucan composition. It is related somehow to Mk 1:40–45 (cf. Lk 5:12–16) and recalls 2 Kgs 5:1–27, the story of the healing of Naaman. The Samaritan story is placed at the beginning of the third part of the journey to Jerusalem. Luke goes out of his way to make the journey and the Jerusalem connections. Since it is difficult to decide the flow of the journey section itself (9:51–18:14), it is also difficult to argue to a particular importance for the story being placed where it is. The analysis of the story in the following pages may yield a reason adequate enough to explain why it is placed here and not elsewhere within the journey, or within the gospel.

One should probably accept vv. 11 and 19 as Lucan casing and vv. 12–18 as a distinct unit within itself. The question as to form is best answered by J. Fitzmyer who speaks of a miracle story which became a pronouncement story.[10] This is a conclusion which imposes itself the more often one studies the rapid and well interwoven thought flow of the first part of the story, vv. 12–14.

In the details of vv. 12–13, one learns of the unnamed village, the encounter with the ten lepers whose marginalized stature is understated in the words "who stood at a distance." The distance is not, however, an obstacle to them. "They lifted up their voices." Is there any particular nuance in their addressing Jesus as "master"? Looked at in terms of a continuum of responses to the presence of Jesus even within the passage, the appellation "master" may indicate the beginnings of a relationship on the basis of human respect, even of recognized authority. To the person who feels marginalized, another seems free, powerful and thus a "master." When a person is thought to be in a position of authority, he or she is often called "boss." It is a communal assessment and denotes social standing. This may explain the plural used in "they lifted up their voices." Jesus has gained social standing both inside and outside the community. The same point may be true of Lk 5:5, where Peter addresses Jesus as "master" as he concedes to lower the nets. "Master, we toiled all night and took nothing. But at your word, I will let down the nets." In the text about the Samaritan, the title "Jesus, Master" also introduces a prayer: "have mercy on us." Fitzmyer notes that "It is an implicit request for help, but whether it would connote a request for alms or a miracle may be debated."[11] The openness of the request leaves the story free to develop in a variety of ways.

New Testament miracle stories exhibit an economy of language and straight narrative lines. Lk 17:14 is a prime example: "when he saw them he said to them, 'go and show yourselves to the priests.' " The verse has three elements:

(a) when he saw them he said to them
(b) "go and show yourselves to the priests"
(c) and as they went, they were cleansed

What moved Jesus to respond to their plight? Did he hear their prayer? Why does the text say: "when he saw them"? Luke trusts that the reader will import the idea of hearing into the mention of Jesus' seeing the lepers. Thus Luke can say the same thing of Jesus in v. 14 as he will say about the one grateful leper in v. 15: "when he saw that he was healed." The first element in v. 14 mentions seeing, assumes hearing and implies understanding or recognition. Jesus recognizes the situation as one pleading for the offer of the kingdom. The one leper in v. 15 recognizes that he is the recipient of a very special gift: the kingdom. What is the source of the leper's recognition? Jesus' response to the question posed by John the Baptist (Lk 7:20–22):

> Are you he who is to come or shall we look for another?
> . . . go and tell John what you have seen and heard
> . . . lepers are cleansed.

The Samaritan counts himself among the "lepers who are cleansed." Attention should also be given in this earlier text in 7:22 to the double command: "go and tell." The change wrought in a miracle has to be demonstrated and the narrative has to be proclaimed. An unproclaimed miracle is a contradiction in terms, and so we are prepared for the second element in v. 14, where there is no mention of any action of healing by Jesus. It concerns demonstration and proclamation.

The second element in v. 14 is the command to go show yourselves to the priests. Why should the lepers go and show themselves to the priests? A similar command in Lk 5:14 carries mention of the intent: "go and show yourself to the priest, and make an offering for your cleansing, as Moses commanded, for a proof to the people." In our text, there is no reason offered for the action commanded by Jesus. Is it therefore a left-over element which now serves the literary purpose of introducing the complication yet to be experienced in the story? The scene in v. 15 supposes that the one leper sets out to go to the priests, recognizes that he is healed and turns back. The command therefore does play an important literary role in advancing the story. But is that all? The command to show themselves to the priests is an indication that now they are readmittable to the community. This is the reason for the visit to the priests. This becomes apparent as the story now focuses on the theme of praise. The community envisioned is the community of praise. What was terrible about leprosy was that a person was kept from participating in the community of the praises of God. To be healed was to be cultically cleansed and to find one's way back into the community.

The third element in v. 14: "and as they went they were cleansed," needs little comment at this point. Jesus speaks no special word of healing. He merely commands. However, what he commands is a courageous and bold step . . . to proceed toward the priests. The emphasis is not on the action of the priests but on the discernment by the lepers of what is happening to them. By leaving a lot unsaid the author focuses attention on what Schneider calls the high point of the narrative.[12] In vv. 15–16, the narrator presents the thankfulness of the healed Samaritan and in vv. 17–19 gives Jesus' response.

The description of this one leper is filled with action words. He praises God in a loud voice. The interspersion of participial forms and active verbs is noted in the following:

(a) one of them
(b) seeing that he was healed
(c) turned back
(d) praising God in a loud voice
(c) and he fell on his knees at Jesus' feet
(b) giving him thanks
(a) now he was a Samaritan

This presentation shows the coordination (b/d/b:participles; c/c:active verbs). The tight arrangement between bc and cb causes the point made in ada to be heard all the more clearly: only one of these cleansed lepers praised God and he was a Samaritan. In these verses, Luke has raised issues important in the passage and indeed issues important in the Gospel and Acts. These verses prepare for the saying of Jesus which comes in the form of questions, the first two of which can be read chiastically:[13]

(a) were not
(b) ten
(c) cleansed
(b) the other nine
(a) where (are they)?

The expectation is that all ten would return. Only one does. On discovering that they were healed, did the others proceed to the priests? Was there only one to return instantly to Jesus without seeing the priest? The new condition in which the leper finds himself justifies the forgoing of Jesus' own command. Such is the alacrity called for by Jesus in one's response to the gift of the kingdom. The priest no longer readmits one to the community of praise; the recipient claims that right in recognition of his new condition. The man threw himself at the feet of Jesus and gave thanks.

What had been specified in v. 16b ("now he was a Samaritan") is expanded in a further question: "were they not found to return to give glory to God except this foreigner?" Jesus' question shows that the story concerns, in a self-conscious way, barriers overcome. In fact, two barriers are overcome in one move. Marshall points out that "foreigner" is found on the "well-known 'Keep Out' signs on the inner barrier in the temple."[14] When that foreigner is also a leper another barrier is taken down. Thus, when a person, leprous and Samaritan, steps forth in praise of what God has done in Jesus, a new world is aborning.

Verse 19 rounds out the episode and gives the nuance which Luke would like the reader to note particularly. "Rise and go" recall the journey motif of v. 11 and may well imply that now the healed leper will accompany Jesus to Jerusalem. "Your faith has saved you." As Marshall notes, this remark doesn't mean that the other lepers did not have faith but that their faith was incomplete.[15] It does not come to expression in praise-filled gratitude. Thus the perfective form of "saved" (*sesōken*) receives its full value. Twice before (7:50; 8:48), and in a scene yet to come (18:42), Luke employs this formula. In 18:35–43, the healing of the blind man near Jericho, the formula is aligned with mention of the man following Jesus and glorifying God; in 7:50 and 8:48, the formula is completed with the dismissal: "go in peace." It would not be off the mark to claim that peace is faith coming to full expression in praise.

The difficulty of knowing the significance of this passage within the narrative of the journey to Jerusalem was mentioned earlier. The reflections on the passage offered above suggest seeing the journey in terms of the place where God is to be praised. Jesus is building an alternative to Jerusalem in calling forth an Israel of praise. Such an enterprise cannot be achieved without many reversals of human expectation, many surprises en route, many barriers overcome. The program, disclosed in the response to John the Baptist (7:22–23), truly gets underway in chapter 14, with the symposium on table fellowship. The story of the Grateful Samaritan contributes mightily to the assembly of the new community of praise of God and of peace for humankind.

Praise is given to God while acts of prostration (respect or worship) and thanksgiving are focused on Jesus in the story of the healed leper. W. Grundmann thinks of a king being honored by these acts[16] and Fitzmyer thinks of Jesus being recognized as God's agent.[17] F. Bovon has addressed the subject of God in the theology of Luke.[18] Bovon claims that Luke did not speculate about God; Luke does not operate on the terrain of metaphysical speculation. He builds himself on an inherited Christian tradition which Bovon states: to know God one needs to pay attention to Jesus. This ancient conviction gets dramatized in Luke. Action speaks louder than words in the prostration of the healed leper at the feet of Jesus. Attention to the person of Jesus as a way to praise God is found in Luke's miracle stories. In a pivotal text (18:37–38) which shall be studied later, all the great works of Jesus elicit the praise of God from the disciples.

Great advances mark the modern study of miracle stories. The literary form has been elucidated in detail by G. Theissen. More importantly, he and others have devoted attention to the interrelationship between form and social setting, the original agenda of the early form critics. Much study has gone into the literary function of the story within a total composition.[19] Our concern here is the issue of the acclamation formula. Theissen works with a definition offered by Klausner.[20] Acclamations are cheers, often rhythmically phrased or uttered in chorus with which a crowd expresses applause, praise and congratulation or rebuke, execration and demand. Verbal comment is the heart of acclamation thus distinguishing it from the motif of wonder which does not disclose what the people said.

There are many examples in Luke where the praise of God is given expression. In the triple tradition of the healing of the paralytic (Mt 9:1–8; Mk 2:1–12; Lk 5:17–26), for instance, while all three mention the glorification by the crowd, Luke alone anticipates the crowd's reaction by having the beneficiary himself glorify God. In the story of the blind Bartimaeus (Mt 20:29–34; Mk 10:46–52; Lk 18:35–43), Luke alone has the important note that the blind man "glorified God and all the people when they saw it, gave praise to God."[21] This praise acclamation which is obviously of great importance to Luke receives special treatment in the passage which we chose as heuristic model for this section of the essay: the story of the Grateful Samaritan.

In an acclamation formula, the claims of the reign of God unleashed in the ministry of Jesus are more clearly recognized. The formula carries a note of competitiveness with the potential of being a battleground for claims and counter-claims. Not all people will recognize a particular event as a deed of God. This is especially so when the event is perceived as an assault on privileged territory, an affront to the establishment. Theissen has done well to explore the motif of limits-overcome which shows up in every miracle story.[22] But one person's limits are another person's defenses. For instance, a person is declared a leper, thus assigned a label in society. His or her limits are clearly underscored. So too are the defenses from getting involved with that person. The deeds of Jesus, and especially the stories told about these deeds, overcome limits for some and defenses for others. There is a new world in the shaping. As we have seen in the story of the Grateful Samaritan, the division is no longer between clean and unclean but between those who give praise and those who do not. Peace is the overcoming of those barriers which had denied one access to the community of praise. The telling of the miracle story is in itself a proclamation of peace. The stories are preserved and used as propaganda.[23] they invite conversion and the resocialization which conversion implies.[24] The point is well made that far more people have been led to faith in Jesus Christ through the telling of those stories than actually experienced the original events. The story as told evokes a whole new world; their recounting engages in what the sociologists of religion call "world construction." The story is told to legitimate this new identity which a person takes on in becoming a member of the Christian movement. The story is not meant to prove anything. It demonstrates what it feels like to belong to this new world opened up in the ministry of Jesus, at once in continuity with the past ("go and show yourselves to the priests") and in radical discontinuity with the zenophobia of a previous age ("except this foreigner").[25] For Luke the greatest barrier to be overcome on the way to peace is the separation of Jews and Gentiles. He devotes particular care to its removal.

Praise and Peace in Missionary Perspective

The story about Peter and Cornelius (Acts 10:1–11:18) shall be our guide in this part of our reflection. Following a study of the story, some attention will be given to the understanding of peace as victory and as achieved through the reversal of human expectation.

The longest narrative in Acts marks a major turning point in the work. All the skill that Luke possessed in storytelling is displayed here; there are repetitions, double vision, speeches and the return of key words and motifs. Especially effective is the retelling of the story (11:1–18) to the Jerusalem audience. The story is first narrated in 10:1–47; the setting is Caesarea and Joppa. Haenchen remarks that the shortened form of the story in 11:1–18, which depends on the longer and more expansive account, is intended for the reader, not really for the Jerusalem audience.[26] In fact, the repeated story is considerably sharpened by the question in 11:3. "Why did you go to the uncircumcised and eat with them?" Peter's reply recalls the double vision, his own objection, the response of the Lord, the arrival in Joppa of the men sent by Cornelius from Caesarea, the experience of the Holy Spirit (vv. 5–16). Luke has thus skillfully underscored all the salient points from his earlier narrative. Many more than the immediate Jerusalem audience hear the all-important question with which Peter concludes: "If God gave the same Spirit to them as he gave to us when we believed in the Lord, Jesus Christ, who was one that I could withstand (*kōlysai*) God?" (11:17). This verse summarizes the concluding section of the original story, 10:44–47, which described the giving of the gift of the Holy Spirit. Lk 11:17 bears a close resemblance with 10:47: "Can anyone forbid (*kōlysai*) water for baptizing these people who have received the Holy Spirit just as we have?"

Peter was in face of an irresistible power whose intention it was to overcome previous barriers. The construction of 10:47 is awkward: "can anyone forbid water . . . ?" Luke wanted to repeat the word *kōlysai* because it expressed very well the barrier being overcome in acquiescing to the will of God twice made known in vision to both Peter and Cornelius. That barrier is described by Peter in 10:28: "You yourselves know how unlawful (*athemiton*) it is for a Jew to associate with or to visit any one of another nation." Sharing a Gentile's hospitality is but one barrier overcome; another barrier is overcome in the refusal to consider anything created by God as unclean (10:9–15); a terribly inhibiting barrier is overcome when one recognizes that no human being is unclean (10:28). These barriers are in reality one barrier, the religious and social separation of

Gentile and Jew which, for both Jew and God-fearer alike, impacted on the construction and maintenance of their respective life-worlds. This is the final and greatest obstacle to fall before the irresistible word of God proclaimed in the early mission of the Christian movement. Peter and his companions discerned that the Gentiles had received the Holy Spirit: "For they (believers from among the circumcised, v. 45) heard them (the Gentiles, v. 45) speaking in tongues and extolling (*megalynontōn*) God" (v. 46). The Gentiles belong now to the community of praise. Peter moves to have these recipients of the Holy Spirit baptized in the name of Jesus Christ. The news of this event recounted in 11:5–17 elicits praise from the hushed audience in Jerusalem: "when they heard this they were silent. And they glorified God, saying, 'Then to the Gentiles also God has granted repentance unto life' " (11:18).

Peter offers his own commentary on these events in his sermon, 10:34–43, which is the highpoint of the first account. The sermon begins with the understanding that God shows no partiality. This is explained further by stating that anyone who fears God and does what is right is acceptable (*dektos*) to him. Verse 36 is translated in the RSV: "You know the word which he sent to Israel *preaching good news of peace* by Jesus Christ." The participle underlined translates *euangelizomenos eirēnēn;* these words refer to God who is seen here as preaching the good news of peace.[27] The sermon develops this assertion by telling how this peace was proclaimed through Jesus. Thus, in v. 38b, the central point is: "he went about doing good and healing all who were oppressed by the devil." In light of our earlier remarks about peace and miracle stories, Acts 10:38b is particularly noteworthy. This notation about Jesus is bound on both sides with affirmations of God's relationship with Jesus. In v. 38a we read: "God anointed Jesus of Nazareth with the Holy Spirit and with power," and in v. 38c "for God was with him." Surely the point of these affirmations is that the same God who worked through Jesus works now through Peter and Cornelius. The peace that God preached through Jesus' good works is one with the peace which is now achieved through the interaction of Peter and Cornelius. Haenchen understands the peace to be that between "God and man."[28] This is insufficient for the context. In light of where Luke places the speech, the peace must mean the new relationship between Jew and Gentile. Moreover, the overcoming of the old antagonism between the two is ascribed to the action of God. The attainment of this peace is celebrated in the chorus of praise in both communities.

The phrase *euangelizomenos eirēnēn* (v. 36) comes from Is 52:7. The text reads:

> How beautiful upon the mountains
> are the feet of him who brings glad tidings,
> announcing peace, bearing good news,
> announcing salvation, and saying to Zion,
> "Your God is King!"

This poem (52:1–12), which Stuhlmueller[29] calls "an enthronement hymn in honor of Jerusalem," proceeds in v. 8 to engage the watchmen who guard the walls of the ruined city in making the good news known. The peace announced is the fruit of victory. Verse 10 is explicit on this point in using an image usually associated with victory, "the holy arm."

> The Lord has bared his holy arm
> in the sight of all the nations,
> All the ends of the earth will behold
> the salvation by our God.

The arm of the Lord is an anthropomorphic symbol of God's power, usually the power which leads Israel to victory over its enemies (e.g. Ex 15:16; Is 51:9; Ps 89:11).

But can we read "peace as fruit of victory" as found in Isaiah 52 into Acts 10:36? Is it sufficient to say that the idea is implicitly present in the participial form *euangelizomenos?* The verb is used twenty-four times in Luke-Acts. Becker claims that the term practically regains "its broader, more Hellenistic meaning of proclaiming good news."[30] However, the proclamation of victory is part of the word's usage. Becker writes: "This verb is the term used in Pss 40:9(10); 68:11(12); 96:2ff. and Isaiah 41:27 and 52:7 to herald Yahweh's universal victory over the world and his kingly rule."[31] Even if one were to agree with Becker that the term in Luke regains its Hellenistic flavor and thus be concerned whether the Old Testament nuance can be promoted for our particular text, it may be noted that the term in our text may come more from the Christian preaching than from Lucan composition. Fitzmyer notes that "because of the syntactic state of the verses, coupled with the allusions to Is 52:7 and 61:1 . . . a reflection of primitive Christian preaching" may be had here instead of a "complete Lucan composition."[32] A celebration of victory was part of the primitive Christian preaching. If Luke does take over these verses, he endorses the theme of victory by naming the actions done by God for the salvation of all. Attention is drawn to God as actor in the flow of the sermon:

v. 34 God shows no partiality,
v. 35 the word whom God sent,
v. 36 (God) preaching the good news of peace,
v. 38 how God anointed Jesus,
v. 40 but God raised him.

Of all these actions, the final one, "but God raised him," speaks most to the theme of victory. In many of the speeches in Acts, this action notes the turning point in the saga of the sinful rejection of Jesus. In a reversal of all that the people did against Jesus, God raised him up. In this action, God claims universal victory. Without this action, there would be no victory. With this action on behalf of the one whom "they put to death by hanging him on a tree" (10:39), the long process of announcing peace is brought to term. Salvation in God, in whom there is no partiality, is available to all. New horizons open up for the Christian mission once this truth is revealed. The missionaries must take their cue from the kind of God to whom they are in service. If this God brooks no partiality then they must show no partiality. The resistance to the universal mission for Jews and Gentiles is overcome when it is revealed that the distinction between Jews and Gentiles does not exist for God.

Peace is victory but the victory is achieved through the reversal of human expectation. This theme of reversal can be discovered in many episodes of Luke's work. It is presented in a programmatic way in Mary's canticle, Lk 1:46–55. There, the ever abiding hermeneutic of the work is announced beforehand. There are differing ways to sort out the flow of the canticle. For our purposes, a two strophic body (vv. 48–50; 51–53) and a conclusion (vv. 54–55) commend themselves. The second strophe is made up of six verbs in the aorist with synthetic parallelism between the verses and antithetical parallelism within the verses:

> He has shown might with his arm;
> he has confused the proud in their inmost thoughts.
>
> He has deposed the mighty from their thrones
> and raised the lowly to high places.
>
> The hungry he has given every good thing,
> while the rich he has sent empty away.

How is the reader to understand these verbs in the aorist? It is not very clear. To be sure, they offer insight into how God is perceived as acting in Mary's life. The primary referent of the canticle is the handmaid of the Lord and in particular the manner in which her child was conceived.[33]

Beyond that, the verbs speak to the wider salvation story. In this framework are the conception and birth of the child to be grasped in faith. The verbs supply the eyes with which one is to view the life of Jesus which will be told; they look to the future of the Christian mission. Schuermann sees them as anticipating the end as already part of the present.[34] Given the importance of the verbs for understanding all that follows, their opening image is all the more significant: "he has shown might with his arm." Fitzmyer alludes to Ps 89:11 where one reads:

> You have crushed Rahab with a mortal blow;
> with your strong arm you have scattered your enemies.

In explanation of the anthropomorphism, Fitzmyer writes:

> (It) is meant to symbolize his strength and power by which
> he reverses the condition in which human beings find
> themselves or which they have fashioned for themselves.[35]

Surely what happened to Mary is a reversal of human expectation. Verse 37 reads: "for with God nothing is impossible." Another barrier has fallen. Is peace at hand? Simeon's prophecy functions as excellent commentary:

> Now, Master, you can dismiss your servant in peace;
> you have fulfilled your word.
> For my eyes have witnessed your saving deed
> displayed for all the people to see:
> A revealing light to the Gentiles,
> the glory of your people, Israel (2:29–32).

Simeon can go peacefully. God, through regard for the lowly handmaid, has already ushered in the overcoming of the final barrier: the Gentiles receive a revealing light and God's own people receive the glory. Both belong to the community of praise. There is peace.

A World Upside Down

The call to follow Jesus, a conversion, is a process of resocialization. One's world is changed. In fact, the experience is often that one's world is turned upside down. If a person's world is considerably changed in shifting from one political party to another, how much more when one realigns the religious meaning of his or her life? When a person joined the community of praise and realigned life according to the gospel of Jesus, each one's conversion changed his or her life-world but also that of family, associates, compatriots, etc. The Christian community is a call to community but each person is called individually. The rite of baptism, already part of the initiation rite at a very early stage, concretized this individual-becoming-community aspect.[36] Christian sources indicate both the conversions of whole households but also the conversion of individuals within households. Often there was much opposition to a person's baptism because it was seen as a threat to another's life-world. Much of Paul's pastoral ministry was devoted to facilitating this transition in his communities. Many of the stories in Acts are also concerned with this construction of a sacred cosmos. The story of how the good news came to Philippi and the story of Simon illustrate this legitimation of world view.

The presentation in Acts 16:11–40 concerns the visit of Paul and his companions to the town of Philippi, the leading city of the district of Macedonia and a Roman colony as Acts is careful to point out. The mission was undertaken at the behest of a "vision appearing to Paul in the night" (v. 9). The stories assembled by Luke tell much about Philippi, the people who live there, their occupations and both the open spirit of some (e.g., Lydia) and the fears of others.

On the power of the word spoken in the name of Jesus Christ, Paul cast the spirit of divination out of a young girl much to the chagrin and financial loss of her owners who stood to gain much from her soothsaying. Her owners seized Paul and Silas and led them to the magistrates with the charge: "These men are Jews and they are disturbing our city. They advocate customs which it is not lawful for us Romans to accept or practice" (vv. 20–21). A fine commentary on these words is found in the following chapter in Acts. In handing over Jason to the authorities, the citizens of Thessalonica indict the missionaries to whom Jason had given hospitality: "These men who have turned the world upside down have come here also" (17:7).

The charge in the Philippi story obviously impressed the magistrates, and Paul and Silas were imprisoned. They were praying and singing hymns to God. Luke makes it clear that the word of God was at work among them; therefore, one may apply the apt saying of 1 Tim 2:9 to the situation of Paul and Silas in Philippi, fettered in the basement of a private household rented by the authorities as a jail: "but the word of God is not fettered." The story served later to explain how a Christian community met in the jailer's house. It met there because that household had unwittingly given hospitality to the irrepressible community of praise. In the same night that the jailer's livelihood and even his life were on the verge of being snuffed out, he and his household were converted to the gospel. So impressive was the earthquake that delivered the disciples, the magistrates moved the very next morning to dismiss the charges against them. "The magistrates have sent to let you go; now therefore come out and go in peace" (v. 36).

These words, "go in peace," translate the customary Hebrew farewell. The NAB overlooks the "go in peace." It translates the phrase: "Get started now on your way." Luke takes the man's conversion into account. Thus we can claim that we have here a Christian farewell. It is the only thread which recalls the conversion of the jailer.[37] The reaction of Paul shows, however, that he judges the compliance of the jailer with his superior's command to be a cover-up. He and his companions have been unjustly detained. They are not going to leave without recognition of their Roman citizenship. Paul complains to the jailer that they are being thrown out secretly and demands a redress of the situation. He is successful. This is clear from v. 39, where it states that the authorities came and apologized to Paul and his companions. "They took them out and asked them to leave the city."

The words "go in peace" lead to this complication and to the eventual redressing of the situation. The matter is not just personal peeve. Luke wants his reader to hear something of the Christian claim for social and legal legitimacy. Paul's later appeal to Caesar is adumbrated in this incident. If "peace" characterizes the Christian way, it is not falsely irenic. The new world which is aborning must be taken seriously. Peace is not just a given; it must be chosen.[38] The wonders worked by God for the benefit of the disciples must be coupled with courageous outspokenness on their part. Both are needed to legitimate the movement. Conversion is resocialization but it does not come about passively. The new life-world of a convert is boldly and actively pursued. The peace released in one's life by entrance into the community of praise is very dynamic and the object of much personal responsibility. This dynamic experience of peace is often marked by zeal and enthusiasm. At times, however, one's entrance into the community of praise can remain subservient to the elements of this world. Think, for instance, of the admonition in Col 2:8: "See to it that no one deceives you through any empty, seductive philosophy that follows mere human traditions, a philosophy based on cosmic powers rather than on Christ." Luke too addresses this failure in the Acts of the Apostles.

The story of Simon in Acts 8:4–24 is a good illustration of an enthusiastic believer who exhibits a great deal of difficulty in leaving behind his outdated way of being in the world. He was a man of immense social standing in the nation of Samaria. He was a magician. He had access to power. "This man is that power of God which is called great" (v. 10). Simon believed and was baptized and attached himself to Philip. He was amazed at the signs and wonders performed. Later, Peter and John came to Samaria to pray for the Samaritans that they might receive the Holy Spirit. "Then they laid their hands on them and they received the Holy Spirit" (v. 17). Simon discovered that the former magician in him had not died. He sought to buy the power to confer the Holy Spirit by the laying on of hands. "Give me also this power, that anyone on whom I lay my hands may receive the Holy Spirit" (v. 19). To Peter's withering reply, as close to cursing as an apostle could come (vv. 20–23), Simon can only reply by asking that Peter's prayer will remain unanswered.

The story concerns the struggle of the Christians with a magical world view. Magic gave Simon access to social power; he was integral to the social structure of the town and its people. The humiliation of Simon was of no small concern if the Christian movement was to receive a hearing; the movement could only gain from his on-going conversion. It was still too much that he remain fascinated with signs and great wonders after his baptism. He could receive the gift of the Holy Spirit but not the power to confer the gift. For him and for his followers their world was turned upside down.

Haenchen notes that Luke's intention "in incorporating the story of the christianized Simon tradition was the possibility of vividly illustrating the superiority of Christian miracles over the magical practices current in the area."[39] Stephen Benko defines magic as "an attempt by human beings to compel a divinity, by the use of physical means, to do what they wish the divinity to do." He further elaborates: "Magic rests upon the belief that by getting hold of demons in physical objects, the divinity can be influenced," thus establishing "a sympathetic relationship with the divinity."[40] Pheme Perkins uses a wider lens when she interrelates astrology and magic. People found out what fate had in store for them through astrology and avoided it through magic.[41] The superiority of miracle over magic of which Haenchen spoke is not, however, to be reduced to a discussion of technique in the production of certain effects. Both miracle and magic are to be viewed on a continuum with regard to technique.[42] Many of the charges made against Christians were precisely that they used magic.

The practices at times looked awfully alike.[43] The difference should be envisioned in terms of the life-world which is being legitimated by a given community in the recounting of either miracle or magic. The life-world that came to expression in Christian miracle was very different from that legitimated by the magical arts.

In the Christian view, life-world is centered in Christ. It is grounded in personal relationship with God. All created reality finds its deepest meaning in its capacity to be used by humankind in symbolizing this relationship with God-in-Christ. The relationship enables one not only to grasp what it is necessary to know for life's journey, but also gives the power to follow through on these insights. In the power of the Holy Spirit, the Christian can deliver on that which is promised in the symbol. Dramatic examples are called miracle stories. They are dramatic but not singular. The daily life of the Christian community is a no less powerful deliverance of the symbolized. Long after the time in and for which Luke wrote, the issues of miracle and magic were hotly debated by the apologists. Magic is the name given to the opponent's miracle. While one denounces the other's miracle stories, one accepts one's own. At times, people in the same camp disputed each other's miracles as magic.[44] This alone indicates that there is something bigger at stake than just the issue of technique. It is the respective life-worlds which are in contention. Despite the widely avowed irenicism of Luke-Acts, a faithful picture of the early Christian movement could not omit the examples of the struggles to maintain the new way of being in the world.

H. C. Kee has done exploratory research in this area.[45] He has traced the use of miracle stories from the end of the Roman Empire to the end of the Antonines. The stories were used in both histories and romances. What we need to underscore is the laudatory character of these stories and the invitation made to later generations to continue praise in the transmission of these stories. The stories become major symbolic representations of the new world evoked and abetted in the memorializations of certain persons. The stories speak of limits overcome and give promise of cosmic harmony and peace. While some stories will speak to an acknowledgment of limits, others will stress the new horizons that can be reached for. The story of Ananias and Sapphira is as important as that of the crippled man who was cured at the Beautiful Gate in Jerusalem. But the stories only come alive in the community of praise on its road to peace. The expression "on its road to peace" is inspired by the closing line in Zechariah's canticle. The image is one of pilgrimage, "process" in modern parlance. So we turn finally to consideration of peace as process.

Peace as Process of World Construction

Many studies have been done on the concept of peace. Eisenbeis and Pedersen are one in upholding the concept of totality.[46] It is central to the idea of *shalom;* the individual situation and context show how this totality or wholeness is present.

What we consider "whole" is quite culturally conditioned. So peace meaning wholeness involves the willingness to negotiate culturally conditioned ambitions and desires. Peace cannot be the sum total of varying understandings which may be exclusive of each other. Peace is God's gift to God's creation when humans seek it in the willingness to negotiate that which is just in a world of limited goods. To speak of universal peace is to express an eschatological hope and is depicted as such in the Scriptures. Only to the extent that Israel perceived itself as instrument of salvation for all the nations do its desires for peace become a universal religious language.[47] Biblical peace is not the preservation of one's own world but the introduction of "a new heaven and a new earth." It is invitation beyond one's stated borders.

A study by Wiseman has shown that the question: "Is there peace?" initiates diplomatic negotiations within covenant making.[48] There is expressed in the greeting-question a willingness to negotiate the terms of an on-going peace. This would be an example of working toward wholeness in an individual situation or context. "Failure to send to ask a king of his peace," contends Wiseman, "was tantamount to a declaration of a state of hostility."[49] The research of Wiseman, to which I will return, dovetails with the understanding of peace presented by von Rad and Schmidt.[50] These scholars speak to the issue of peace as social reality and social process.

Considerations along this line suggest possible meanings in a number of Luke's uses of the peace symbol.

Mission Protocol

The word *eirēnē* occurs three times in Lk 10:5–6. In v. 5 it is part of the greeting. "On entering any house, first say, 'Peace to this house.' " It is an offer of the kingdom. This is stated clearly in v. 9: "the kingdom of God has come upon you," and in v. 11 this is a fact realized even by those who refuse. "Nevertheless, know this, that the kingdom of God has come near." "Peace to this house" is as powerful a greeting as the words of Jesus to Zacchaeus: "today, salvation has come to this house" (Lk 19:9). This offer of peace cannot be refused with impunity. Many commentators note that this is no ordinary greeting.[51] Schneider notes correctly that the peace greeting is an imposition of peace for those who are the sons and daughters of peace.[52] The very offer sets up a whole new relationship in the life of the individual greeted. The peace greeting is interrogative in intent if not in form. The greeting seeks to know whether there is a willingness to peace or not, a willingness, an openness to the gift of salvation. It seeks to know if the final barrier to the entrance of the kingdom into people's lives can be overcome: their own resistance to the favor (*eudokia* v. 21). The reader is plunged into the depth of the God-human relationship. The grace to overcome the resis-

tance is itself gift. But will it be accepted? Jesus, on hearing of
the marvelous response to the preaching of the disciples (vv.
17–20), leads the chorus of praise given to God (vv. 21–22).

In v. 6, the word *eirēnē* is used twice where the greeting
is followed up by a process of discernment. "If there is a peace-
able man (or woman) there, your peace will rest on him (or
her); if not, it will come back to you." The phrase *huios eirēnēs*
was studied by W. Klassen in the context of the first century.[53]
Klassen is prepared to accept that the formula, which he translates as "child of peace," goes back to Jesus himself. "For Jesus," he writes, "the child of peace is one who has been born
of peace and is also destined for the peace of others."[54] Many
commentators accept the idea that the formula means "destined for peace."[55] H. K. Luce notes that the child of peace is
"one who is worthy to receive the peace from God which the
missionaries pray that he may receive."[56] This insight of Luce
is very helpful in understanding the greeting. It is not merely
interrogative; it is also a prayer that the evangelized will become a messenger of peace also. The greeting comes out of a
community of prayer, the missionary community of praise
which sends out and receives back the itinerant missionaries.
The child of peace is confronted with a design of love on his
or her behalf. The offer is immensely attractive; it comes with
the power of Jesus and is the moment of Satan's futile last
stand. It is a victory spurned by the wise but accepted by
"babes" (v. 21).

Luke is as clear on peace as human responsibility as he is
on peace as gift of God. Openness to the peace greeting is in
fact openness to the call to discipleship. That call is heard in
the midst of one's home life. Discipleship is no escape from
the world; the call to peace is in the midst of one's world, in
the household, the mediating structure between the individual and the world. Luke is aware of the disruptiveness which
this gift of peace will bring about and thus obviously reflects
many situations in the early Christian communities for which
he is writing (cf. Lk 12:49–53). This experience of tension is

no justification for retiring the Christian mission. It means only that the gift of peace is such that one is enabled by the giver of the gift to cope with the resistance. "Nevertheless do not rejoice in this, that the spirits are subject to you; but rejoice that your names are written in heaven" (Lk 10:20). Like a good pastoral guide, Jesus sets the experience of the disciples in a wider context. He opens them up to interpret their experience in terms of the eschatological horizon. The new world into which they are ushered was long sought for by kings and prophets. It can be revealed by one who is Son. The apocalyptic vision sets the disciples in the presence of the Father, Lord of heaven and earth.

Jerusalem: City of Peace

Lk 19:41–44 presents Jesus drawing near to Jerusalem and weeping over the city. The material which is probably pre-Lucan[57] is fitted into the flow of the context in a number of ways. It was prepared for by v. 37[58] which telescopes the movement of Jesus at the descent of the Mount of Olives and the reaction of the multitude who are rejoicing and praising God. An atmosphere of dénouement is engagingly presented in the verse. Ernst notes the prophetical character of v. 40.[59] If the disciples are refused their song of salutation (v. 38), the very stones will cry out (v. 38) as in fact they did under Titus in 70 A.D. (v. 40). For our purposes, the occurrences of *eirēnē* in vv. 38 and 42 are important. The first we can read as divine gift:

> Blessed is the king who comes in the name of the Lord!
> Peace in heaven and glory in the highest.

In the first line Luke is citing Ps 118:26 to which he adds the word "king." Jesus comes as a king bringing peace. The second use of the word *eirēnē* (v. 42) indicates human responsibility. Fitzmyer translates the verse:[60]

> Would that you, even you, had recognized this day
> what would make for peace!
> But, as it is, that is hidden from your sight.

The translation "recognized" in place of the word "known" is particularly happy because it evokes an evaluative cognition of the peace process. God has visited his people (1:68, 78; 7:16; 19:44) in the ministry of Jesus. When one responds to Jesus, one recognizes the gift who is peace. Fitzmyer's translation also captures the pathos of the verse: "Would that you, even you, had recognized. . . . " The pathos now is that the recognition of what makes for the fulfillment of the promise of peace comes along only in the refusal to accept Jesus. That long refusal will have its final hour (cf. Lk 22:53). Ernst writes:

> In the messianic entrance of Jesus into Jerusalem, God offers salvation to his people one last and definitive time but the decision is already made; the rejection by the inhabitants of Nazareth finds its ratification in the holy city of Jerusalem.[61]

If there is a journey to discipleship there is also a journey to refusal. For this reason the NAB translation of v. 42 is helpful: "If only you had known the path to peace. . . . " The introduction of "path," although not literally in the text, does build a warranted connection with 1:79: "the path of peace." John Donahue suggests reading the journey section of Luke's gospel as the path to peace.[62] The vision of Jerusalem as a city of peace fulfilled by the presence of Jesus is the goal of the journey and the point of departure for new journeys of both Jesus and the disciples (Acts 1).[63] It is a journey marked by lament. The note struck in 19:42[64] echoes the lament of Jesus over Jerusalem (13:34–35) and anticipates the lament of the women of Jerusalem (23:27–31).

In the earlier passage 13:34–35, in the apostrophe to Jerusalem, Jesus' overtures to the city are spurned. In the lament itself there is no reason given why the city rejects Jesus' love and concern. But the immediately preceding verse (v. 33) upholds the necessity that Jerusalem rejects the prophets.[65] De la Potterie has studied the two spellings of the word "Jerusalem" found in Luke.[66] He claims that here the sacred name (*Ierousalēm*) is used. This is a promise of salvation. The children of the city will one day acclaim Jesus with the cry of welcome: "Blessed is he who comes in the name of the Lord" (13:35; Ps 118:26). De la Potterie argues that the future lot of Jerusalem is part of the salvific plan of God. The community of praise will survive on the other side of lament only because God will make it live.

The second passage, 23:27–31, which relates to this lament of Jesus over Jerusalem concerns the women of the city weeping for Jesus on his way to be crucified. The passage ends with a question which is easier to answer than to know of whom it is asked: "If they do these things in the green wood, what will happen in the dry?" Fitzmyer reviews many opinions and opts for the following: "If God allows the innocent Jesus to suffer such a fate as Jerusalem prepares for him, what will be the fate of Jerusalem?" ("The damp, soggy wood, difficult to kindle" burned first.)[67] The matter is all the more sorrowful because it even defies the ways of nature. But the question remains open. The call to repentance is all the more urgent.[68]

These two passages seem to intensify the sense of lament in the scene of Jesus' coming to Jerusalem. The protasis of 19:42 without an apodosis opened the passage to such reflection. The tension between lament and praise is held but lament will ultimately give way. It is hoped that the barrier to peace, before which the lament is painfully raised, will eventually collapse. The praise given to God will endure even if the stones must echo it. Where is that praise coming from? It is the accumulated acclamation of the entire ministry of Jesus: "the whole multitude of the disciples began to rejoice and praise God with a loud voice for all the mighty works that they had seen" (19:37).

In a short exposé on Ps 100, W. Brueggemann wrote: "our

world is not an easy place for doxology but praise is permitted by our faith. Where such praise is practiced the world is made new."[69] Praise is permitted by our faith! In face of the awful lament over Jerusalem, the presence of the community of praise gives immense hope. In his study of the Psalms,[70] Brueggemann develops at much greater expanse the meaning of lament and praise. In dialogue with the sociologists of religion, his "postcritical" approach to the Psalms delineates three general interconnected themes: orientation, disorientation and new orientation around which themes it is possible to group the Psalms. There are then two decisive moves of faith: "one move is out of settled orientation into a season of disorientation." The other is a move "from a context of disorientation to a new orientation." The moves are never once-for-all. The second move is from lament to praise but with a whole new sense of urgency and frailty. Under psalms of new orientation, Brueggemann discusses "the once and future king."[71] These Psalms about "new kingship of Yahweh" are "the songs of new orientation par excellence." This brief presentation of Brueggemann's work sets a stage in which to draw together the elements of this study.

"If you want peace, work for justice." So go the very memorable words of Paul VI. To those I would add "work for justice in, through and with a community of praise." For our first task in doing the things which lead to peace we take our cue from those who accompany Jesus to Jerusalem: create a community of praise out of the telling loudly and publicly what good things God does on our behalf. The ministries of justice and peace run the risk of burn-out, even of distortion unless supported and sustained by a community of praise. And such a community gives these ministries the small-size, person-oriented, conscience creating human dimension which they need and in which alone they will work. Luke works on world visions but in the dimensions of household communities of praise. The Samaritan with leprosy, the jailer in Philippi, Cornelius: they all accepted to join in the praises of God of peace.

In this call to peace, there is not only the invitation to the community of praise, there is also the launching of a new way of being in the world. So the community need not be understood in a privatized, inward-looking way; rather, it is public, open and directed to mission. This makes the terrain to be struggled for all the more public and exposed. The vision of Luke is: "think globally, act locally."

NOTES

. .

1 H. Conzelmann, *The Theology of Luke* (New York: Harper and Row, 1961); J.A. Fitzmyer, *The Gospel According to Luke I–IX*, Anchor Bible, vol. 28 (New York: Doubleday, 1981 and 1985), pp. 3–29; W.M. Swartley, "Politics or Peace (Eirēnē) in Luke's Gospel," in R.J. Cassidy and P.J. Scharper, eds., *Political Issues in Luke-Acts* (Maryknoll, N.Y.: Orbis Books, 1983), pp. 18–37.

2 For discussion of the breakdown of the verse, see Fitzmyer, *Luke I–IX*:410–12.

3 C. Stuhlmueller, "The Gospel According to Luke," in R.E. Brown, J.A. Fitzmyer, and R.A. Murphy, eds., *Jerome Biblical Commentary* (Englewood Cliffs, N.J.: Prentice-Hall, 1968), 44:42.

4 See R.J. Clifford, "The Hebrew Scriptures and the Theology of Creation," *Theological Studies* 46 (1985):507–23.

5 R.J. Cassidy, *Jesus, Politics and Society: A Study of Luke's Gospel* (Maryknoll, N.Y.: Orbis Books, 1978), pp. 1–19.

6 "Luke was a theologian who artistically wove together the component threads of theology—history (tradition), apology (the present situation), and eschatology (hope). Imbedded in his historical narrative was a clear message to the church, an *apologia pro imperio*, which would help the Christian community live effectively with the social, political, and religious realities of the present situation until the advent of God's reign." (P.W. Walaskay, *"And so we came to Rome": The Political Perspective of St. Luke* [London: Cambridge University Press, 1983], p. 67.)

7 P.-E. Bonnard, "Le Psaume 72: Ses relectures, ses traces dans l'oeuvre de Luc," *Recherches de science religieuse* 69 (1981):259–78.

8 Ibid., 277.

9 W. Brueggemann, *The Message of the Psalms* (Minneapolis: Augsburg Publishing House, 1984), pp. 142–43. Brueggemann makes a connection with Lk 2:14: "The movement from glory (vv 1–2, 10) to peace (v 11) is not unlike the angel song at Bethlehem (Lk 2:14). The establishment of the new king brings with it new well-being to the world. The action of the psalm is to sing into place the new order that overcomes chaos" (ibid., p. 143).

[10] J.A. Fitzmyer, *The Gospel According to Luke X–XXIV*, Anchor Bible, vol. 28a (New York: Doubleday, 1985), p. 1150.

[11] Ibid., p. 1154.

[12] G. Schneider, *Das Evangelium nach Lukas*, Oekumenischer Taschenbuchkommentar zum Neuen Testament 3/2 (Guetersloher: Wuerzburg, 1977), p. 350.

[13] I.H. Marshall, *The Gospel of Luke*, New International Greek Text Commentary (Grand Rapids: Eerdmans, 1978), p. 652; Fitzmyer, *Luke X–XXIV*, p. 2:1155; W. Grundmann, *Evangelium nach Lukas* (Berlin: Evangelische Verlagsanstalt, 1978), p. 337.

[14] Marshall, p. 652.

[15] Ibid.; see the explanation of the obedience of the nine lepers, but also their failure, by Fitzmyer, *Luke X–XXIV*, p. 1155.

[16] "Nach arabischer Anschauung erfordert Heilung von Aussatz des Standescharisma von Konigs" (Grundmann, p. 337).

[17] Fitzmyer, *Luke X–XXIV*, p. 1155.

[18] F. Bovon, "Le Dieu de Luc," *Recherches de science religieuse* 69 (1981):279–300, especially 283.

[19] G. Theissen, *The Miracle Stories of the Early Christian Tradition* (Philadelphia: Fortress Press, 1983).

[20] T. Klausner, "Akklamation," *Reallexikon für Antike und Christentum* I:216–33, 216 cited by Theissen, p. 71. See his remarks, pp. 71–72, 152–73.

[21] Luke's emphasis on the people is important in this verse in view of the impending division between leadership and the people which will take place in Jerusalem. See J. Comblin, "La paix dans la theologie de Saint Luc," *Ephemerides theologicae lovaniensis* 32 (1956):439–60.

[22] The point is made repeatedly in Theissen. He discusses it both under motif and under theme. "Faith is therefore not just one motif among other motifs of boundary crossings associated with human characters, but the essence of all motifs of boundary crossings" (p. 139). "What seems to me unique is that here faith means an act by which a human being crosses a boundary in the face of actual suffering as an answer to a revelation which challenges a human being in his totality" (p. 140). See also D. Senior, *Healing as Boundary Breaker: The Cross Cultural Impulse of Early Christianity*, Institute for World Concerns (Pittsburgh: Duquesne University, n.d.).

[23] E. Schüssler Fiorenza, "Miracles, Mission and Apologetics: An Introduction," in E. Schüssler Fiorenza, ed., *Aspects of Religious Propaganda in Judaism and Early Christianity* (Notre Dame: University of Notre Dame Press, 1976), pp. 1–25.

[24] A.D. Nock, *Conversion: The Old and New in Religion from ALexander the Great to Augustine of Hippo* (London: Oxford, 1933).

[25] H. Bietenhard, "foreign," in C. Brown, ed., *New International Dictionary of New Testament Theology*, vol. 1 (Grand Rapids: Zondervan, 1975), pp. 686–89; G. Stahlin, "xenos," in G. Kittel and G. Friedrich, eds., *Theological Dictionary of the New Testament*, vol. 5 (Grand Rapids: Eerdmans, 1967), pp. 1–36.

[26] E. Haenchen, *The Acts of the Apostles* (Philadelphia: Westminster, 1971), pp. 355 and 357.

[27] Many authors note the difficulty with the syntax of this speech. The difficulty is particularly obvious in vv. 36–37. R.P.C. Hanson writes: "The grammatical looseness reaches its apogee in this verse which has been smoothed out in the RSV translation" (*The Acts* [Oxford: Clarendon, 1967], p. 124).

[28] Haenchen, p. 352 n. 2.

[29] C. Stuhlmueller, "Deutero-Isaiah," in R.E. Brown, J.A. Fitzmyer, and R.A. Murphy, eds., *Jerome Biblical Commentary* (Englewood Cliffs, N.J.: Prentice-Hall, 1968), 22:42.

[30] U. Becker, "gospel," in C. Brown, ed., *New International Dictionary of New Testament Theology*, vol. 2 (Grand Rapids: Zondervan, 1976), p. 113.

[31] Ibid., p. 109.

[32] J.A. Fitzmyer, "Acts of the Apostles," in R.E. Brown, J.A. Fitzmyer, and R.A. Murphy, eds., *Jerome Biblical Commentary* (Englewood Cliffs, N.J.: Prentice-Hall, 1968), 45:58.

[33] J. Dupont, "Le Magnificat comme discours sur Dieu," *La nouvelle revue théologique* 11 (1980):321–43.

[34] H. Schurmann, *Das Evangelium nach Lukas* (Freiburg: Herder, 1969), p. 75.

[35] Fitzmyer, *Luke I–IX*, p. 368.

[36] See M. Green, *Evangelism in the Early Church* (London: Hodder and Stoughton, 1970).

[37] Haenchen, p. 498.

[38] E. Judge remarks on the struggle for legitimation in "The Decrees

of Caesar at Thessalonica," *Reformed Theological Review* 30 (1971):1–7.

[39] Haenchen, p. 308.

[40] S. Benko, "Magic and divination," in P.J. Achtemeier, ed., *Harper's Bible Dictionary* (New York: Harper and Row, 1985), pp. 594–96.

[41] P. Perkins, *Reading the New Testament: An Introduction* (New York: Paulist Press, 1978), p. 114.

[42] S. Benko, "Magic and Early Christianity," in *Pagan Rome and the Early Christians* (Bloomingdale: Indiana University Press, 1984), pp. 103–39.

[43] H. Remus, *Pagan-Christian Conflict over Miracle in the Second Century* (Cambridge, MA: Philadelphia Patristic Foundation, 1983), pp. 48–72.

[44] Ibid., pp. 73–82.

[45] H.C. Kee, *Miracle in the Early Christian World: A Study in Sociohistorical Method* (New Haven: Yale University Press, 1983), pp. 174–220.

[46] W. Eisenbeis, *Die Wurzel Shalom im Alten Testament*, Beiheft zur Zeitschrift für die alttestamentliche Wissenschaft, vol. 113 (Berlin: de Gruyter, 1969); J. Pedersen, *Israel: Its Life and Culture*, vol. 1 (London: Oxford University Press, 1926), pp. 263–335.

[47] For example, Is 2:1–5; 8:23–9:6; 11:1–9. Note the developmental approach to the question of war and peace in the Scripture section of the pastoral letter, "The Challenge of Peace: God's Promise and Our Response," *Origins* 12/44 (April 1983):697–728.

[48] D.J. Wiseman, "Is It Peace: Covenant and Diplomacy," *Vetus Testamentum* 32 (1982): 311–26.

[49] Ibid., 317.

[50] G. von Rad and W. Foerster, "eirēnē," in G. Kittel and G. Friedrich, eds., *Theological Dictionary of the New Testament*, vol. 2 (Grand Rapids: Eerdmans, 1964), pp. 400–19; H.H. Schmidt, *Shalom: Frieden im Alten Testament* (Stuttgart: Katholischer Bibelwerk, 1971).

[51] J. Ernst, *Das Evangelium nach Lukas* (Regensburg: Pustet, 1977). He notes that "the peace greeting of those sent by Jesus is not just an empty phrase of politeness but an expression of eschat-

ological salvation which will be granted to people as a divine gift" (p. 333).

52 Schneider, *Lukas* 1:237. He further describes people of peace as "those for whom it is appointed."

53 W. Klassen, "A Child of Peace (Luke 10:6) in First Century Context," *New Testament Studies* 27 (1981):488–506.

54 Ibid., 501.

55 For example, Marshall, p. 420; Fitzmyer, *Luke X–XXIV*, p. 848.

56 H.K. Luce, *The Gospel According to Luke* (London: Cambridge University Press, 1949), p. 199.

57 Marshall, p. 717.

58 Fitzmyer, *Luke X–XXIV*, p. 1253.

59 Ernst, p. 528.

60 Fitzmyer, *Luke X–XXIV*, p. 1256.

61 Ernst, p. 530.

62 J. Donahue, "The Good News of Peace," *The Way* 22 (1982):88–89.

63 E. Rasco, *La teologia de Luca: Origen, Desarrollo, Orientaciones* (Roma: Universita Gregoriana, 1976), pp. 118–22.

64 Fitzmyer, *Luke* 2:1256.

65 *Ouk endechetai* is translated "it will not do," with the further comment, "the idea of necessity enters in," by F. Rienecker and C. Rogers, *Linguistic Key to the Greek New Testament* (Grand Rapids: Regency, 1976), p. 182; Marshall claims that the verb "suggests the appropriateness of death in Jerusalem" without producing the "false general rule that all prophets perished there." The recurrence of the theme of necessity in Luke warrants the reading of the text in reference to Jesus. See further F.D. Weinert, "Luke, the Temple and Jesus' Saying about Jerusalem's Abandoned House (Luke 13:34–35)," *Catholic Biblical Quarterly* 44 (1982):68–76; also Weinert, "The Meaning of the Temple in Luke-Acts," *Biblical Theology Bulletin* 11 (1981):85–89.

66 I. de la Potterie, "Les deux noms de Jérusalem dans l'Evangile de Luc," *Recherches de science religieuse* 68 (1981):57–70.

67 Fitzmyer, *Luke X–XXIV*, p. 1498; the description of the wood as "damp, soggy, etc." is also his.

68 Grundmann, p. 430: the prophetic word is a call to repentance.

69 W. Brueggemann, "Psalm 100," *Interpretation* 39 (1985):65–69.

[70] W. Brueggemann, *The Message of the Psalms*. See also his "A Shape for OT Theology I: Structure and Legitimation," *Catholic Biblical Quarterly* 47 (1985):28–46, and "A Shape for OT Theology: Embrace of Pain," *Catholic Biblical Quarterly* 47 (1985):395–415.

[71] Brueggemann, *Message of Psalms*, p. 140.

Chapter Five

PRINCIPALITIES, POWERS AND PEACE

. . . . . .

Anthony J. Tambasco

When one considers the social foundations for peace, it seems an obvious conclusion that one must consider the nature and the role of the principal social institution underlying activities of war and founding times of peace, namely, the state. Social activity and social involvement to further the cause of peace will one way or another have to reckon with governmental authority as a positive or a negative force. While the biblical text does not and cannot give a specific program of action, it can offer perspectives and horizons which define genuine Christian activity. This paper will deal with one limited area of biblical material which seems fruitful for gaining insight into the nature and role of the governing authorities and the Christian's position in reference to these institutions. The paper will discuss the role of principalities and powers, especially within the Pauline texts.

Three Hermeneutical Approaches to the Powers

Once again, in considering these texts, we need to be mindful of presuppositions which we bring to the reading of the material, and we need to seek an ever-widening horizon which moves us out of our own limited perspectives or world view. Such hermeneutical considerations help to move us beyond the treatment of principalities and powers as typified by Rudolf Bultmann.[1] His major concern was with treating these concepts as indicative of a pre-scientific age, and as in need of demythologization. For Bultmann the only reality expressed by these concepts was a personal and existential reality. They typify the threat of sin and rebellion against God, and their continued existence even in a Christian world shows that sin continues to menace the Christian. There is, however, also the mythological concept of Christ dethroning the powers, indicating that ultimately sin need not rule and that ultimately the threat to Christian existence can be repulsed.

Bultmann's treatment of the topic has several salutary features. The fact that the powers are part of God's creation and are always subordinate to God is a strong refutation of Gnostic dualism. There is also in this approach a healthy emphasis on human responsibility. Paul is not interested in cosmic speculation, but in how human beings react toward that cosmos, i.e., in the ramification of the power of sin on the human situation. As Hendrikus Berkhof has indicated, Paul speaks of the existence of these powers and also of their influence on human affairs. The apostle clings less to the former fact and more to the latter.[2]

These points of Bultmann are related to a typical question asked by exegetes about the powers: Did Paul actually believe in the existence of spiritual powers as personal realities, and if he did, do we have to? Exegetes agree with variations that Paul adapted his view of principalities and powers from the Old Testament angelology combined with Greco-Roman astrological concepts. The Greek astral deities, the *daimones*, are no longer deified, but are interpreted in terms of the Jewish concept of angels.[3] Some scholars, however, think that Paul begins to depersonalize these powers. He seems less interested in these powers as personal beings than in their influence on human creation. Berkhof says, "We must set aside the thought that Paul's 'Powers' are angels."[4] Thus Paul seems to speak more of personifications than real persons. Be that as it may, the end conclusion is that even if Paul did believe in personal beings, we do not have to. As D.E.H. Whiteley words it, "I personally believe . . . there *are* no principalities or powers, but St. Paul employs this language to express something which is both true and important."[5]

What is true and important has too often been associated simply with the fact of sin and the present threat of evil which must be overcome by the Christian. This view returns us to the personalist and existential perspective of Bultmann. Our hermeneutical concerns have shown the shortcomings of such a view alongside the advantages. It reduces the Scriptures to one philosophical school of thought, it does not allow enough room for the social and communal dimensions of Christian faith, and it underestimates in many ways the reality contained within mythical language. Recognition of these shortcomings has no doubt been influential in the development of another interpretation of principalities and powers parallel to the existentialist view. This interpretation puts a stress on these powers as symbolic of the social and political institutions of the world.

Whiteley seems to come at this view by distinguishing the meaning of the powers in Paul from that of the powers in the Gospels. He says that the demons in the Gospels are seen as causes of sickness of individuals and are related to what we would now categorize as medical or psychological evils. The principalities and powers in Paul, on the other hand, are universal threats related more to what would concern politicians, sociologists and others.[6] The presence of Satan in the temptation stories as a power who possesses the kingdoms of the world, or in Peter who wants to throw out Roman rule after Caesarea Philippi, makes one cautious about too sharp a distinction between Paul and the Gospels, but Whiteley does have a fruitful point about the powers being associated often enough with political institutions.

G.H.C. Macgregor opts for the same thing by saying, "Paul has in view demonic intelligences of a much higher order than the 'devils' who possessed the poor disordered souls that meet us in the Gospel pages. These are *cosmic* spirit forces which possess and control not only individual human lives but the very course of the universe."[7] This exegete extends his thought by making explicit recommendation of Oscar Cullmann's relating of these cosmic dimensions to the state. Cullmann's thesis has the merit of maintaining the spiritual reality of the powers, while advocating their worldly sphere of activity in the state. According to Cullmann, Paul's description of the powers as spiritual beings enables the apostle to situate the state within a context of salvation history. The state is not merely a secular reality, but comes somehow under the reign of Christ. This kind of language also enables the apostle to place the state within an eschatological context. By showing the control of the powers as essentially broken but not yet completely eliminated, Paul explains the ambivalent attitude that the Christian has toward ruling authorities, both supporting them and criticizing them. Conversely, this spiritual/political duality of the powers in eschatological context also accounts for why the state's decisions of good and evil can both converge with and diverge from the Christian's ethical judgment.[8]

While Cullmann's thesis has the merit of stressing social dimensions of biblical faith and of moving beyond simple existentialist categories, one wonders whether it adequately understands the nature of the mythical language involved. Cullmann seems concerned with the spiritual dimensions of the powers mostly to ground a theological vision of human political institutions. Once that vision is defined there seems no further use for principalities and powers. In other words, Cullmann's presentation is another form of demythologizing which implies that the meaning of myth is exhausted in its rational explanation. Once again, recent hermeneutical considerations have brought us to recognize that mythical language brings meaning which captures a reality irreducible to empirical or scientific experience. Any demythologization requires a remythologization in order to keep the full meaning of a text.

Walter Wink has published two volumes of a three-volume work which attempts to reconsider the principalities and powers in a way that more fully respects the vital meanings contained in the mythical language.⁹ He begins with the salutary point that the ancients and the biblical authors themselves understood myth in a more sophisticated fashion. Because we rely so heavily on scientific and empirical evidence, we see as the only alternative a spiritual and naively unscientific view which we then impose on the ancients. We think the ancients conceived of and believed in the spiritual world in the same way that we conceive of and disbelieve in it. Wink would propose, instead, a third possibility, that the ancients had an imaginative knowledge of a world that is "real yet unsubstantial, as actual spirits having no existence apart from their concretions in the world of things."¹⁰ In other words, the powers are not persons in a world apart from the material, but neither are they only symbols of a purely material reality. They are real, immaterial, invisible dimensions of the concrete manifestations of power in human history.

In what follows in this essay we will continue to consider the principalities and powers as biblical myth for the political and social institutions in human history. However, we will follow the lead of Wink in seeing that these powers are more than just the external structures and systems. In Wink's terms, we will see the myth as capturing the fact that there are an inner and an outer aspect of any manifestation of power. "As the inner aspect they are the spirituality of institutions, the 'within' of corporate structures and systems, the inner essence of outer organizations of power. As the outer aspect they are political systems, appointed officials, the 'chair' of an organization, laws—in short, all the tangible manifestations which power takes."¹¹ With that lead, we will consider what Paul tells us of the nature and role of the state in his description of principalities and powers.

The Pauline message in this regard revolves around a dozen or so passages. These are: Rom 8:38–39; 13:1–3; 1 Cor 2:6–8; 15:24–27; Gal 4:3,8–11; Col 1:16; 2:8–10,20; Eph 1:20–23; 2:1–2; 3:10; 6:12. Scholars have debated whether the texts refer to earthly or heavenly realities in the first place. Where they have found reference to heavenly realities, then they have frequently demythologized the texts in personalist terms or more frequently in terms referring to political institutions. The debate over whether the terms are earthly or heavenly has strong arguments on both sides. In the long run, however, the only reality intended is the visible, human institution, whether directly or through mythical symbolism. Perhaps more is going on in these texts. Wink suggests that the irresolubility of this problem indicates that the texts more likely speak of both earthly and heavenly realities at the same time. One text may highlight the human political institution, and another the heavenly realities behind this institution, but either emphasis always has the other lurking in the background. Moreover, the heavenly descriptions are present precisely to describe another dimension of the empirical, political institutions, namely, the invisible, but real characteristics which inhere in these earthly realities.[12]

The Powers in Reference to Government

Assuming correctly that these texts refer to both empirical and deeper dimensions of human institutions, we can now examine in more detail the nature of these institutions. G.B. Caird has indicated that Paul's treatment of principalities and powers refers to three main institutions, the Roman religion and government, the Jewish law, and the area of nature itself as the arena of human action.[13] That there is some relationship of the powers to Roman authority seems clear enough from Rom 13:1–7. The powers are said to wield the sword (power of coercion of the state?) and to levy taxes. Victor Furnish observes, in fact, that the point of the entire passage is to get the Roman Christians to respect civil order by paying both direct and indirect taxes levied upon them.[14] Now both the sword and taxation are the prerogative of earthly rulers of government, so that the powers are therefore related to government.

But Paul gives civil authority a deeper dimension by seeing it as controlled by heavenly powers. In 1 Cor 6:3, he says that Christians ought not to bring their lawsuits to civil judges and then says that the Christians will judge the angels behind these judges. In Eph 6:12, he contrasts the principalities and powers with flesh and blood, so that there is a deeper dimension to the "world rulers of this present darkness" than is visible in the human beings who exercise the power. What might this deeper dimension be? Wink suggests that it is the spirit of political and social institutions which have a life of their own beyond the individuals who form the institutions. "It is clear that we contend not against human beings as such ('blood and flesh') but against the legitimations, seats of authority, hierarchical systems, ideological justifications, and punitive sanctions which their human incumbents exercise and which transcend these incumbents in both time and power."[15]

The use of many different Greek words to describe the powers highlights in itself the suprahuman dimensions of institutional power beyond the mere individual human agents. On the one hand, the many different words are interchangeable or at least synonymous. But the juxtaposing of several of the words after each other in one passage (e.g., Col 1:16; Eph 6:12) gives the impression of the universal and comprehensive nature of the powers, which makes them difficult to narrow down to one visible dimension.

On the other hand, in spite of their interchangeability the various words for the powers have nuances that again show the diffusive nature of political institutions and power. For instance, *archē* and *archōn* are used almost always to indicate the agent of power, the incumbent in office. *Exousia* is used generally to indicate the authorization to exercise power, i.e., political legitimation, ideological justification, etc. *Thronos* emphasizes the actual seat of government, the continuity of power resident in but also beyond the incumbent. *Kyriotēs* has the nuance of the realm or expanse of territory in which power is exercised. We can use all the words to speak of power, but the nuances show the complexity of power. Power cannot be equated simply with the person in power, because persons can be replaced. Power is not simply in the legitimating rationale, because that needs to be given its authority by something else. Power is not simply in a role, for persons fill roles differently. Power, therefore, can only be adequately understood as the convergence of many elements, and as a reality that transcends any of its visible manifestations.[16]

One of the traditional questions that has been asked about the powers is whether they are seen by Paul as only evil. While someone like Alan Richardson believes that Paul has no good angels in his epistles,[17] most exegetes would point out that Paul stresses that even the principalities and powers are created in Christ (Col 1:16), and that once again the risen Christ is head over every rule and authority (Col 2:9–15). The problem with the powers is in between their creation and their ultimate conquest. Paul is heir to an entire tradition that speaks of this time in terms of the fall of the powers, their rebellion against God, setting up a rival dominion that refuses subordination to God. Exegetes have commonly understood this as the absolutizing of power by human authority, and the yielding on the part of citizens to the dictates of human authority so that it becomes the object of ultimate allegiance.

Seeing a deeper, invisible reality within the human institutions, we might speak of distortion of the systems, ideologies, and patterns within which power operates. These become oppressive instead of instruments at the service of God's will for the world. Joseph Weber has shown how the powers become demonic in the sense that social structures enter into a dialectical relationship with the persons establishing them, so that the structures come to have a reality of their own which becomes internalized and shapes the very humanity in which it had its basis.[18] The process is almost an automatic usurpation of authority by the very structures which are necessary for human existence and organization. Political institutions have nothing intrinsically evil about them and are necessary for human community even in the best of worlds. But these structures which are intended to serve human community begin to dominate human beings and to establish themselves as ultimate. This takes place subtly and surreptitiously during the course of day to day living. Eph 2:2 says the prince of power can also be called the "power of this air." Paul is not referring to spirits in the sky, but to the atmosphere within which we live, the context of daily living which dominates thoughts, attitudes and actions. The rest of the verse shows that this air is characterized by disobedience, a rebellion against God, a claiming of absolute rather than instrumental position in the world. We can describe this invisible reality as a being overcome by public opinion, peer pressure, institutional expectations, false patriotism, etc.[19]

This rebellion leads to death, the last of the enemy powers (Eph 2:1; 1 Cor 15:26), which in Paul's understanding means separation from God. To treat human institutions as ultimate and to live by the spirit of these institutions necessitates cutting oneself off from the very source that gives life and meaning. Nevertheless, death is not final and Christ conquers these powers. The victory over the powers is treated by Paul within his twofold eschatological teaching of Christian life "between the ages." Christ has already conquered the powers in essence (Eph 1:20–23), although the full effects of that conquest have yet to be unfolded (1 Cor 15:24–27). The manner in which Christ conquers the powers is described by Paul as an exposing of the pretensions to absoluteness and ultimacy of these powers.[20] In Col 2:13–15 he describes Christ as having a victory procession in which the powers are paraded as public spectacles totally disarmed of their oppressive power. In 1 Cor 2:6–8 the death of Christ exposes the ignorance of the powers. Human power, jealous of its authority, saw Christ as a threat to the institutions and put him to death. Christ's death and resurrection shows God's redemptive concern for human beings which neutralizes the oppression of people for the sake of the status quo. These rulers are "doomed to pass away."

The victory is not complete and the powers have dominion still, but their power is broken. Paul says it well in Rom
8:38–39: *no* power (and the juxtaposing of many words for
power shows the comprehensive dimensions of that power,
both visible and invisible), even if it still seeks to impose its
authority, can separate from the love of God. If we interpret
this language as pointing to the invisible realities behind the
visible institutions of power, we can say that Christ's witness
of love and redemption has conscientized people and given
them an inner freedom. The ideologies, public pressures, internalized legitimations of unjust human structures have been
exposed and their demise begins. They still rule, and they
cause suffering. They have yet to be eliminated. But no
amount of torture or state sanction, no public opinion or police
practice can remove from an individual the sense of self-worth
and the dignity of one's human person in Christ. The victory
is not complete, but it has already begun with the witnessing
of God's love for each in the person of Christ.

This view of the powers indicates several conclusions for
the attitude of the Christian toward the governing institutions.
First of all, the Christian does not seek to eliminate political
structures and authority. Being created in and for Christ, these
structures can serve as an instrument of Christ promoting human dignity and freedom. There are at present, however, unredeemed elements in these structures whereby they are a
source of oppression rather than freedom. The Christian faces
these elements, invisible as well as visible, with a sense of
hope. This does not mean that the Christian can do everything
about reforming these institutions, but neither does it mean
that he or she can do nothing. Some Christian sects say that
the Christian life is separate from involvement in the world,
that the unredeemed powers continue to operate in the world,
but that Christians have been freed from these powers and witness as counter-community. If we consider, however, that
Christ has already conquered the powers in some ways, that
they are part of redeemed creation and are not eliminated, and

that they will exist in subordination to Christ in his kingdom (Col 2:9–10), then part of hope is that human political institutions can be reformed and that Christians must work actively within the human institutions to transform them.

One reason why some Christian sects strongly insist on leaving government within its own limited sphere is the biblical teaching that Christ, not Christians, will redeem the powers. This is certainly a central truth. However, overemphasis on this truth can lead to distortion, since Christ works in and through the Christians, and Christians need to respond to what Christ offers as gift. A passivity toward the powers, leaving them to the work of Christ, runs the risk of simply maintaining the status quo of the society. In many ways, it becomes actual support for the oppressive structures of the society, for not to decide against the powers is to ultimately decide to accept them. Our distinction between the visible and invisible dimensions of human institutions, however, may help to clarify the issue we are discussing. There are powers that only Christ can change, namely, the spirit or the invisible realities behind human institutions. Christians can at best reform the external and visible structures of the institutions, and hope that this will lead to a change of spirit, but only God can bring about the deepest changes. Ideologies cannot be eliminated by fiat. Conscientization can expose them, and changes of human institutions can challenge oppressors toward inner change. But ultimately faith and prayer are needed to ask God for the final transformation.[21]

The Powers in Reference to Law and Creation

To this point we have considered the powers as indicative of deeper realities behind the human institutions of the state and political authority. We have now to look briefly at the two other institutions which Paul also identifies with the powers, the Jewish law and nature as the arena of human action. In Col

2:13–15, Paul says that Christ, through his death on the cross, conquers the powers by cancelling the record of our infractions with its legal demands. This is reminiscent of Gal 3:13, where Paul says that Christ freed us from the curse of the law. The meaning is that law is able to make us guilty of sin but is unable to free us from it. In many ways the law shares in the same fate as structures of government. Both were created good and intended to serve God's will. Both still have a God-given function, but now take on a fallen condition. Because of sin political institutions become oppressive. Because of sin, the law does not move us to the good, but simply removes our ignorance and imputes guilt.[22] But Paul personifies the law in the same way that he personified governing authority. He speaks of the law as part of the principalities and powers. Why? Our answer as before must recognize the nature of myth as capturing a specific reality and not simply as indirect reference to the same reality known without myth.

Paul refers to the powers behind law to express an invisible and deeper reality which pervades law and legal institutions, i.e., the imaging of law as the basic explanation of life and action. In this regard law, like political structures, has a tendency to claim ultimacy and absolute authority. What is secondary in God's will claims primacy. So, in Paul's vocabulary, what was given by the angels becomes demonic. This same point is made in those texts where Paul speaks of the powers as "elemental spirits of the universe," the *stoicheia tou kosmou* (Gal 4:3,9; Col 2:8,20).

Stoicheia can have many meanings, but they all revolve around the concept of something basic or fundamental, e.g., the ABC's, the four elements of the universe in early Greek philosophy, or the constituent elements of something. When Paul uses the term in Galatians he refers to the Jewish law, not insofar as it is a series of rules or practices, but insofar as it is a foundational view of life. This view has claimed ultimacy, has become demonic, and is being conquered by Christ. The Galatians are warned not to return to such powers, once having been freed from them. It is interesting to note in Galatians that Paul is writing to Gentile Christians. In telling them that their turning to the law is a return to the *stoicheia tou kosmou,* Paul makes the point that the Gentile religious beliefs were themselves a basic world view which claimed absolute authority and became demonic.

He reaffirms the point in Colossians 2, where the *stoicheia* as religious beliefs in verse 20 are joined to the *stoicheia* as philosophy about the foundations of the universe in verse 8. In all, Paul speaks of an invisible reality behind all law, science, and religious practice as having a life of its own and as needing to be subordinate to God's will. As Wink sums it up, the term "focuses on the problem of idolatry. What is most basic to existence begins to be worshiped, either overtly or, as more often happens, unconsciously, as people abandon themselves to religious practices or philosophical ideals or ideological principles. . . . The *stoicheia* become functional gods."[23] In revealing the genuine basis of creation and in supplanting law and Gentile religious practice, Christ has reduced these powers to "weak and beggarly elements" to which we ought not return.

We can see a complicity between political authority and religious beliefs and philosophies of life, sometimes with each reinforcing the other, sometimes with rivalry between them. In either case there is the demonic element as they mutually or competitively seek absolute dominion and ultimacy. Paul does not make radical distinctions between all these elements when he speaks of the principalities and powers, because Christ must rule over all. We might now add that Paul also weaves into his image of the powers the effects that these human institutions and structures have on nature itself. Paul seems here to deal with the Greek sense of the organic unity of nature and with the Greek concern for immortality. The widespread sense of meaninglessness among the lower classes of the empire and the turning toward the mystery religions to overcome the threat of death gave a sense that creation itself

was in rebellion. Paul had a sense that even in this search for
the meaning of creation people were turning in the wrong directions and giving ultimacy to the wrong powers. Creation itself had been subjected to futility (Rom 8:20), so that it no
longer fulfilled the purposes for which God brought it into existence. It had become demonic.[24]

If we see the personifying of creation itself as a power in
the same way that we saw the personifying of political authority and basic philosophy of life, we can say that Paul wants here
as well to talk of an underlying invisible dimension to our life
in creation. We might say that creation is good or bad only in
relation to human decisions affecting it. The reality that un-
derlies our particular acts of stewardship over creation is a basic
ecology, a basic view of the purposes and uses of creation. Humanity has plundered creation, made it an end in itself or a
means to selfish ends, and distorted its position as mediation
of the divine. In that way creation seems controlled by principalities and powers. In that sphere also Christ frees from
these powers. He himself provides the principle of cohesion
and unity within the universe and the goal toward which all
tends (Col 1:16). Ultimately he shows that all creation is to
bring humanity to unity with God, so that nothing in all creation, neither height, nor depth, nor any other creature will separate from the love of God (Rom 8:38–39).

Our paper began with the desire to relate the theme of
principalities and powers with that of peace. Some of that
point is clear enough even if implicit in what has been developed. We conclude this paper with some suggestions regarding
the social foundations of peace. Peace depends very much on
the relationships between nations, which in turn depends very
much on the images the nations portray to themselves, their
individual citizens, and the other nations. Much is bound up
with the hidden realities behind visible state structures, the
ideologies, the legitimations, the systems that infuse the authorities and their decisions. Paul's teaching cautions us to be-
ware of these realities claiming ultimacy. Making application

to particular ideologies and systems goes beyond the biblical
text, and debate is legitimate when one tries to name the powers specifically in the world today. However, the biblical text
does encourage us to name the powers. One that surely needs
attention is the ideology of national security. It is a power that
transcends political systems and is accepted today as ultimate.
It creates an impasse that frustrates any further movement
toward disarmament and that perpetuates the status quo. It has
a legitimacy, but it is not ultimate. Paul might very well suggest to us today that the ideology of national security is demonic and needs conquering. Nations are not ultimate, so
neither is *national* security.[25]

Another important social foundation for peace is justice.
Paul's teaching on the powers might alert us here to the in-
transigency of economic structures which become demonic.
Laws of economics might also have complicity when they become obstructive of justice. Basic economic world views might
be blind to further realities, and might cause further injustice.
One economic presupposition of the first world merits looking
at, to see if it is not a demonic structure, an obstructive law or
world view. It is the economic theory of development, i.e.,
that the underdeveloped countries are simply in a second
round of development, following the already developed countries. Latin Americans protest that development is not a fact,
but rather dependency. They are surely underdeveloped, but
they are not developing, and as long as the presuppositions remain in place that they are, the poor will get poorer and the
rich richer.[26] Again, there may be debate in applying Paul to
the specifics of laws as powers, but this economic law needs
some challenging. Papal teaching has certainly moved from
development theory to a keener sense of dependency between
rich and poor nations.

Finally, the relationship that Paul develops between the
powers and creation itself may lead us to another social foundation for peace, namely, the ecological concerns of the world
today. More and more scientists and physicians speak out

against war and call for peace. Nuclear armaments have brought us to a new kind of world situation in which creation itself is affected by human decisions for war. Perhaps Paul calls us to further reflection on the environment and the tasks of science and technology in a new age. Perhaps a growing awareness of the demonic element in the technological imperative, the process by which technology pulls itself forward without control, can work for peace more than direct action on the political level. In any case, Paul reminds us that even technology is not the ultimate, that you do not have to do it because you can do it.

If our study has achieved anything, it has at least shown that Paul's teaching on principalities and powers is not simply a study in demythologizing a quaint pre-scientific world view. Paul has a deeper sense of the power of evil which needs consideration even in our own age. It is a mythology for the twentieth century and beyond. But Paul also offers in this mythology the ultimate hope of Christian faith. Christ has conquered the powers.

NOTES

· ·

1. Rudolf Bultmann, *Theology of the New Testament*, vol. 1 (New York: Charles Scribner's Sons, 1951), pp. 257–59.
2. Hendrikus Berkhof, *Christ and the Powers* (Scottsdale, Pa: Herald Press, 1962).
3. G.H.C. Macgregor, "Principalities and Powers: The Cosmic Background of Paul's Thought," in Harvey K. McArthur, ed., *New Testament Sidelights: Essays in Honor of Alexander Converse Purdy* (Hartford: Hartford Seminary Foundation Press, 1960), pp. 88–104.
4. Ibid., p. 19.
5. D.E.H. Whiteley, *The Theology of St. Paul* (Philadelphia: Fortress Press, 1972), p. 20.
6. Ibid., p. 19.
7. Macgregor, pp. 90–91.
8. Oscar Cullmann, *The State in the New Testament* (New York: Charles Scribner's Sons, 1956), pp. 95–114.
9. Walter Wink, *Naming the Powers: The Language of Power in the New Testament*, vol. 1 of *The Powers* (Philadelphia: Fortress Press, 1984), and *Unmasking the Powers: The Invisible Forces That Determine Human Existence*, vol. 2 of *The Powers* (Philadelphia: Fortress Press, 1986).
10. Ibid. 1:4.
11. Ibid. 1:5.
12. Ibid. 1:40–50.
13. G.B. Caird, *Principalities and Powers: A Study in Pauline Theology*, The Chancellor's Lectures for 1954 at Queen's University, Kingston, Ontario (Oxford: at the Clarendon Press, 1956).
14. Victor Paul Furnish, *The Moral Teaching of Paul* (Nashville: Abingdon, 1979), pp. 115–141.
15. Wink, 1:85.
16. Ibid. 1:13–22, 108.
17. Alan Richardson, *An Introduction to the Theology of the New Testament* (London: SCM Press, 1958), p. 209.
18. Joseph Weber, "Christ's Victory over the Powers," in Thomas

Clarke, ed., *Above Every Name: The Lordship of Christ and Social Systems* (New York: Paulist Press, 1980), pp. 66–72.

19 Heinrich Schlier, *Principalities and Powers in the New Testament* (New York: Herder and Herder, 1961), pp. 30–32.

20 Caird, pp. 84–88.

21 Wink, 1:126–27.

22 Caird, pp. 39–53.

23 Wink, 1:77; see also 1:67–77.

24 Caird, pp. 72–75.

25 See Gerald and Patricia Mische, *Toward a Human World Order: Beyond the National Security Straitjacket* (New York: Paulist Press, 1977).

26 Franz Hinkelammert, "The Economic Roots of Idolatry: Entrepreneurial Metaphysics," in Pablo Richard, ed., *The Idols of Death and the God of Life* (Maryknoll, N.Y.: Orbis Books, 1983), pp. 165–93.

Chapter Six

THE EARLY CHRISTIAN TRADITION ON PEACE AND CONFLICT RESOLUTION

. . . . . .

Robert J. Daly, S.J.

Most of the material contained in this paper can be found treated at greater length in several previous publications.[1] I have synthesized, abbreviated and recast it for the purposes of this presentation. The principal purpose of this chapter is to consider the dialectic that takes place between the world view of the early Christians, who presupposed their community to be a minority within society, and the world view of modern day Christians who see their community as more widely spread in the world. This dialectic is joined to others, e.g., the pacifist/just war assumptions brought to the biblical texts, the difference between war in the past and nuclear war today, etc.

The New Testament

The theme of peace is richly represented in the Bible and early Christianity. So too is conflict resolution, as long as one does not try to project back into history our modern understanding of the term. This history has been richly and diversely interpreted, so diversely in fact that proponents of every conceivable position from radical pacifism to a hawkish crusader mentality have claimed the Bible for support. Either one must find a more objective way of reading the Bible, or give up on it as a resource for judging the authenticity of various Christian positions. Fortunately, biblical scholars have attained an impressive level of methodological consensus about the main lines of critical biblical interpretation. However, the same claim cannot be made for the history and literature of the patristic period. This massive body of data has yet to be subjected to the same detailed scrutiny. Thus, what I have to say about the early church will be far more hypothetical than what I have to say about the New Testament.

If one takes the three attitudes of pacifism, just war and crusade commonly used by modern writers,[2] and asks which of them is supported by the New Testament, most exegetes agree in their answer. But first, a vitally important distinction must be made. "Pacifism" has religiophilosophical and political connotations which are difficult to verify in the New Testament and early church. It is far sounder to speak of nonviolence as embodying the central gospel message, and not to identify it uncritically with pacifism. This said, the summarizing conclusion drawn by René Costé over twenty years ago is still valid:

> It is an incontestable fact that Christ *did* preach nonviolence, both as a condition and a consequence of the universal love that he taught us. To pretend, as is sometimes done, that his directives are only meant to be applied to individual or ecclesial relationships is a supposition that is nowhere justified in the writings of the New Testament.[3]

As clear as this statement is, and we are assuming a great deal of detailed exegesis to affirm it, it still leaves us a long way from home. How was this ideal understood and lived in the early church? One sometimes hears the claim: the early Christians were nonviolent; therefore we must be nonviolent too, if we are true Christians. Those who make such claims usually do not realize how badly they are discrediting the ideal of nonviolence. I am not arguing with the conclusion, mind you. But it simply does not hold *as* a conclusion from *this* premise. First of all, one cannot argue from what the early Christians were to what modern Christians must be without the mediation of a critical hermeneutic. After all, early Christians apparently believed in the morality of slavery, and no one takes that belief to be normative for today. Secondly, and most damagingly, the fact presumed in the premise, "the early Christians were nonviolent," simply cannot be proved historically. There is, in fact, significant evidence which suggests the opposite, evidence which historians who do not read history with a pacifist bias can easily marshal into a convincing case that, the teaching of Jesus notwithstanding, the early Christians were apparently no more successful in living out the ideal of nonviolence than Christians of other ages. Nonviolence is too valuable a Christian ideal to allow it to be undermined by the support of shoddy, easily demolishable arguments.

One way to provide the ideal of nonviolence with valid support is to examine the way the New Testament call to nonviolence is rooted in the so-called love command ("so-called," because, strictly speaking, love cannot be commanded).[4] The three key texts for our purposes are from Matthew's Sermon on the Mount, Mt 5:38–48, the parallel passage in the Lukan Sermon, Lk 6:27–36, and the Epistle to the Romans 12:14, 17, 19–21. In these verses from Romans we read:

> Bless those who persecute you; bless and do not curse. . . . Repay no one evil for evil. . . . Beloved, never avenge yourselves, but leave it to the wrath.

This was written by Paul in the late 50s. The Matthaean and Lukan passages which talk in a similar vein about loving one's enemies give evidence that this was a constant strand in New Testament teaching. The New Testament authors were handing on something they obviously believed to be at the very heart of Jesus' message. As we examine this material, several critical questions arise: What did it mean? How did the early Christians understand it? What does it mean for us now? These are not, as modern biblical scholarship has come to see, identical questions.

Remember, there are two aspects to the love command: the positive aspect of loving one's enemies, and the negative aspect of nonviolence or of not resisting evil. But does this, as the existential interpretation following Rudolf Bultmann would have it, refer just to what goes on internally in the heart of the one who loves; or does it also, and especially, look to the effect that nonviolence will have on the heart of the enemy? The answer is fairly clear. Only the latter answer, that the love command looks to the conversion of the enemy, to the effect on the heart of the enemy, does justice to these texts in their full context. This sees love of one's enemy as a concrete social event. Thus, sociological analysis is absolutely necessary.

> One should note however, that this is not a universally applicable ethical rule, but the attitude expected of Christians when they encounter resistance. It can be practiced only by the weak toward the strong. Only those involved in the resistance of the weak toward the strong can preach or demand it. When it is recommended or imposed from outside, it is perverted into a demand to give up resistance.[5]

The first question raised by this analysis is: Why are both the positive and negative elements of the love command (love your enemies—resist not evil) always found at all levels of the New Testament tradition? What did these early Christians mean when they combined a renunciation of resistance to evil along with an active love of enemy?

Non-Christian antiquity knew several examples of nonresistance: (1) the magnanimous or politically expedient renunciation of revenge by the powerful; (2) the philosopher's nonviolent acceptance of abuse in order to proclaim the rottenness of society; (3) the attitudes and reactions of the powerless underdog. Only this third situation fits that of the early Christians. Further, if we are thinking of application to current situations, we have to recognize that we are in murky waters:

No early Christian source pays any attention to the social situation of dependence that gave Christians no other option but to submit to injustice peaceably. Thus, the question on this level remains open: Is this a universal ethic for everyone, or only for Christians in a similar situation of powerlessness?[6]

Further analysis confirms that all levels of the New Testament tradition understand loving one's enemies in the active, even aggressive, sense of a missionary attitude toward enemy and persecutor. It was an appeal to bring them into the Christian fold, make them one's brothers and sisters in the Lord. *This gives the love command a public and implicitly political dimension because it explicitly refers to the identity of social groups.*[7]

Disappointingly, this brings us to the end of what one can confidently conclude from the reasonably sure methods of biblical exegesis. We are not going against exegesis, but we are going beyond what it can strictly prove, we are moving into the less clearly charted waters of patristic interpretation and early church experience when we claim that these texts seem to apply

specifically and concretely in the area of politics, especially insurrectional or revolutionary politics. Christian are not revolutionaries, but they do resist evil. The prohibition is not a fundamental rejection of every type of resistance. In fact, as Tertullian put it, Christians are, precisely because they are Christians, factors of resistance in society (Tertullian, *Apology* 37). They resist injustice, driven by an aggressively missionary love that impels them by nonviolent yet active means to try to bring all, including the persecuting enemy, into the fold of Christ.

If this is so, it relativizes somewhat the NT call to nonviolence and its modern political counterpart, pacifism. It locates the absolute, nonnegotiable center of the Christian message in the positive call to love and not in its negative counterpart and normal mode of realization, nonviolence. This does not imply, for example, that the just-war theory is equally well grounded in the NT as is nonviolence. But it does suggest that one cannot a priori assume that any attempt to observe the love command which does not live up to the ideals of nonviolence is necessarily a betrayal of the gospel.[8]

Is there a balance we can draw from this New Testament witness, any Christian guidelines or principles for peacemaking and resolving conflict? I think we can say that the New Testament commits Christians to be active rather than passive, to have what one could call an aggressive, missionary attitude toward removing the grounds for conflict by bringing the enemy into the Christian fold, that this has both social and political ramifications, that the heart or empowering source of this "program" is Christic, self-giving love, and that the essential or characteristic mode of its realization is nonviolent.

But a great deal remains open, e.g., how aggressively should Christians push their missionary activity when they know that such activity will precipitate violent reactions? And most significantly, this "program" was preached as a way of life by and for those who were, politically and socially, an insignificant, powerless minority, and who seem to have left us no reflection on this sociological context of their teaching. What is to be the Christian program when Christians are no longer a powerless minority? History shows that, through the ages, most Christians, in their own cultural and political situations not directly envisioned by the gospel, have not tried to apply the New Testament teaching literally. But critical historical and theological reflection also exposes a general Christian lack of success in developing social and political programs that were both appropriate to their own situations and also in continuity with the obvious teaching of the New Testament. Once Christians realized that the gospel teaching could not be transferred literally, without remainder, without interpretation, to their own situations, they have all too readily absolved themselves from its transforming call to love one's enemies and to bring them, lovingly and nonviolently, into the fold.

The Early Church

If we take the four centuries from the time of Jesus to the death of Augustine in 430 A.D., we can see the Christian church moving through five distinguishable phases: (1) the founding years up to the end of the first century; (2) from the Apostolic Fathers up to Origen in the first half of the third century; (3) from the mid-third to the beginning of the fourth century; (4) the time of Constantine and Eusebius in the first third of the fourth century; (5) the phase of "establishment" reflected in the careers and writings of Ambrose and Augustine at the end of the fourth and beginning of the fifth centuries.

We can also identify three themes that endured, with mostly minor variations, through these five phases: (1) an attitude toward the value of human life; (2) the appropriate function of war; (3) the superhuman or divine element in military power and warfare.[9]

The first phase was basically that of the New Testament described in the first part of this paper. It was the experience of being a new community struggling to grow out of its Jewish background and struggling to become itself in the much broader Greco-Roman context of the Mediterranean world.

The second phase was the time when, up to the first half of the third century,

> Irenaeus, Tertullian, Hippolytus, Cyprian, Clement and Origen were setting the foundations and framing the structures of Christian theology. During this time, Christians knew themselves, socially and politically, as an insignificant and powerless minority struggling to establish its identity and existence in an inhospitable and sometimes downright hostile world.[10]

Let us touch down at four points in this second phase.

(a) The fascinating story of the *Legio XII Fulminata*, the Thundering Legion, is recounted by both pagan and Christian sources (although each told it in a way to glorify its own religion). As told by the Christian writers (Tertullian in his *Apology* a few years after the reported event and Eusebius some one hundred and fifty years later), this legion was fighting under Marcus Aurelius against the Germans and Sarmatians on the Danube frontier when it got trapped without food and water. The soldiers were dangerously weakened when Christians in the legion prayed for deliverance. Immediately a rainstorm blew up that both provided water and put the enemy to flight with bolts of lightning. Regardless of how historical the story may be, what is significant for us is that the Christian sources tell the story with pride. There is not the slightest suggestion of embarrassment about Christians being in the army.

(b) Tertullian, apart from his apologetic use of the story of the Thundering Legion in *Apology* 37, was an inveterate opponent of Roman military service. Despite the fact that he describes it as a Christian duty to pray for the emperor and his armies, he remained an inveterate opponent of Roman military service. The *Treatise on Idolatry* and the *Treatise on the Crown* explain why. It was practically impossible for a Christian in the army to escape involvement in the idolatry and immorality that pervaded and surrounded Roman military life. All of Tertullian's strictures against the military are in this religious context. None of them are in the context of what we would call pacifism or the Christian ideal of nonviolence. In fact, Tertullian has no clear statement on these at all. Nothing from his considerably extensive writings suggests that pacifism or nonviolence was important to him.

(c) The canons from the *Apostolic Tradition* of Hippolytus of Rome from the early decades of the third century also put the occupation of the military in the context of idolatry and immorality and condemn it on that basis.[11] There is nothing in the text to suggest support for an early Christian pacifism. This is the only place in all his writings where Hippolytus even mentions military service, and he makes no reference whatever to a prohibition of a soldier killing in combat while in the line of duty. Hippolytus was a rigorist moral teacher whose rigorist views subsequently led him into schism before his eventual reconciliation and martyrdom. This suggests that the ideals of pacifism or nonviolence were not prominent in the thinking of early third century Christians in Rome.

(d) Origen of Alexandria (d. 251) has been touted as the first Christian pacifist theorist. Actually, it is more accurate to say that he is the first Christian thinker to give serious reflection to the matter. Carefully following the norms of evangelical morality, he teaches that Christians are never allowed to use force, take up arms, or kill, even in self-defense. In his eight books *Against Celsus* (A.D. 248), a refutation of Celsus' work from about A.D. 178, Origen admits the pagan charge that Christians refuse to serve in the army. However, this does not, as Celsus charged, make them delinquent in their duty to support the works of peace, justice and public order; for Christians are a priestly people whose task it is to fight evil only with spiritual means:

> . . . How much more so, that while others are engaged in battle, these too should engage as the priests and ministers of God, keeping their hands pure, and wrestling in prayers to God on behalf of those who are fighting in a righteous cause, and for the king who reigns righteously, that whatever is opposed to those who act righteously may be destroyed! And as we by our prayers vanquish all demons who stir up war, and lead us to the violation of oaths, and disturb the peace, we in this way are much more helpful to the kings than those who go into the field to fight for them (*Against Celsus* 8.73).

Origen envisioned a world in which war and violence would progressively disappear in proportion to the spread of Christianity. He viewed war or the use of force to resolve conflicts as a pre-Christian or sub-Christian activity that will become obsolete as the world becomes Christian. Thus Christians must not, cannot, get involved in such things. Origen's vision did not come true, and probably never will in any foreseeable future. His vision was of little help to later Christians who had to face the question he assumed a Christian would never have to face: whether or how force could or even should be used to bring about justice and peace? Actually, one can trace the beginnings of the medieval two-sword theory back to Origen.[12] Despite his massive commitment to Christian pacifism and nonviolence, he actually set the stage for the Christian just war theory.

The third phase spans the years from the end of the persecution of Gallienus in the middle of the third century to the beginning of the persecutions of Diocletian and Galerius in the beginning of the fourth century. This is a phase much neglected by scholars who have reflected on this material. This is unfortunate, because it is key to understanding that what happened later at the time of Constantine was not a massive reversal of early Christian teaching and practice, but a fairly natural consequence of what had been developing for some time. In terms of Christian persecutions, this period has been described as one of peace. One might more accurately see it as a time of testing. The empire and the still fledgling Christian community had apparently begun to perceive each other as rivals. The relative tolerance of the empire may well have been due to the hope that Christianity, if left to itself, might just fade away. But increasing numbers of Christians apparently found place in public life and even in military life. The stage was set for the great confrontation when Diocletian and Galerius tried to strengthen the empire internally by imposing religious uniformity. By the time Constantine recognized Christianity as a valuable ally in the pursuit of his own political ambitions, Christianity was still a minority but, quite obviously, no longer insignificant or powerless. The sociological setting of Christianity had irrevocably changed.

It was within this period that one finds most of the authentic, pre-Constantinian Acts of the Military Martyrs. There are some half dozen of these accounts, most of them from North Africa, which give in protocol form an account of the incidents that led up to, and the trials that ensued, when

Christian soldiers were delated for being Christian, or got fed
up with the religious compromises of their military life. Strik-
ingly, not once is the theme of pacifism or nonviolence mentioned. Quite the opposite, one Christian soldier mentions in
his defense that he always did his duty bravely in the front line
of battle.[13] It was their rejection of the pagan religious aspect
of the soldier's life that got these Christians into trouble, not
any difficulty with the violent duties of the soldier's profes-
sion.

The early Christian apocryphal literature that was beginning to form at this time is also revelatory. Dismissed by scholars as containing a crude and vulgar theology that did not do
justice to the gospels, it is only recently that these writings
have been accorded their place in helping us to draw a much
more pluralistic picture of early Christian life. It may be too
much to claim them as key sources for studying popular religious psychology among early Christians, but they are not insignificant. They portray the boy Jesus as arbitrarily using his
divine powers to turn clay sparrows into real birds, and to kill
the playmates who offend him, or the teacher who disciplines
him.[14] Such stories, which were very popular and get repeated
in this apocryphal literature, seem to be the expressions of a
powerless, illiterate people which fanaticized retribution, the
kind of person who often has a special attraction to the military
way of dealing with conflict. They clearly do not represent the
best of early Christianity, but it would be foolish to ignore
them, just as it would be foolish in our own day to ignore the
television soaps as expressions of popular American culture.

The fourth phase, in the early fourth century, is identified
with the names of Constantine and Eusebius. Modern Christians tend to be embarrassed at the glorified role that church
leaders like Eusebius attributed to Constantine in the history
of salvation. Part of this is due to our neglect of what was going
on in the third phase. With that in mind, one can see beyond
the polemical and apologetic excesses of a Eusebius and see
what happened after Constantine's accession as a fairly natural

development from what Christians were experiencing and reflecting on throughout the previous century. Concerning Eusebius, the first Christian whom one might call a "court theologian," three points can be made.

(1) Eusebius, bishop of Caesarea from ca. 315 to ca. 340 A.D., was first and foremost a Christian *apologist*. The primary purpose of his *Ecclesiastical History*, which he finished in A.D. 323, was to pour Roman facts into a Christian framework.

(2) With reference to military matters, Eusebius wrote loyalty in large letters throughout his work. Here are some of his important points culled from the way he writes the history of the Thundering Legion in Book 5 of the *Ecclesiastical History:* (a) Christians are loyal to the empire. (b) Their loyalty has positive consequences for the empire. (c) Good emperors favor the church while bad or incompetent ones, such as Verus, cause the church grief. (d) There was no criticism of those Christians serving in this legion or any other. Nothing is said which might suggest that Christians fought less effectively than other Roman soldiers.

(3) Eusebius takes special care to fit Constantine into the framework of the theme of the *divine king*. In classical views, the emperor was thought to be the one who made the connection between heaven and earth. In so doing, the king, or emperor, brought salvation, interpreted as a series of material and social blessings, into the empire. Eusebius elaborates this theme by viewing the emperor as the ensoulment of the cosmic order: the emperor is to the state as God is to the world, a kind of cosmic liturgy.[15] Constantine, as he killed off each rival, became increasingly closer to the earthly icon of God's monarchy. Eusebius writes of this in apocalyptic fashion. The victory of Constantine meant that the end times were close at hand. It was the time, too, for the apocalyptic destruction of the demons, for they especially were responsible for leading the bad emperors to persecute the Christians. Constantine sweeps all before him because he is a "friend of God"; all those who oppose him are God's enemies.

There was also support for Constantine in the West. In August 314, the Synod of Arles apparently tried to aid Constantine by making sure that Christian soldiers stayed in the army. Its canon 3 reads:

> Concerning those, who throw down their arms in time of peace, we have decreed that they should be kept from communion.[16]

Christian soldiers who disarm themselves in peacetime, the military martyrs and those inclined to follow their example, are the ones most likely meant, for the army units would not automatically stop being hotbeds of idolatry and immorality just because Constantine came to power. This may have been the first instance of Christian church authorities encouraging or enjoining individual Christians to remain in military service against their consciences.

The fifth phase, that of "establishment," is reflected in the writings of Ambrose and Augustine. In the late fourth century, the church seems to be making a transition from the toleration granted by Constantine to establishment.

Ambrose, bishop of Milan, applied scriptural images of the Israelite kings to the Roman emperors. He did this particularly in his description of the victory of Theodosius, the pro-Christian emperor, over Eugenius, the pro-pagan usurper in 394. The whole victory, which Ambrose extols in his *Commentary on Psalm 37*, is glorified as a victory of Christ over the demons, of true religion over false religion.

Augustine of Hippo developed a theory of the complementarity of the earthly and heavenly cities which legitimated the waging of war by Christian rulers. Augustine's famous correspondence with Boniface, a military commander in North Africa, establishes the Christian military vocation on the twin commands of love of God and neighbor. Bodily strength and military skill are divine gifts to be dedicated to the service of God's people in helping them to attain that earthly peace which foreshadows the eternal peace of the kingdom of heaven.[17] About 425, Augustine wrote his fullest consideration of war and peace in Book 19 of *On the City of God*. From Augustine come many of the major elements of what we now call the just war theory.

Throughout these five phases, as we mentioned, we can find three themes, enduring with but minor variations.

The first theme: attitudes toward human life and property. The destruction of human life and property does not seem to have been a significant consideration for either Christian or pagan. Augustine even explicitly rejects it as a religious consideration. For some, like Origen, this may have been due to an antimaterial bias, or the belief that the present order was but a temporary one to be transformed or replaced at the return of Christ. Others considered bodily death or material loss as due punishment for sin, or a necessary travail on the path toward glory with Christ. The early Christians, with few exceptions, seemed to see no lasting value in the achievements of the dominant pagan culture, nor did they mourn their destruction in warfare.

The second theme: the appropriate function of war. The basic attitude toward the purposes and justification of warfare seemed to be remarkably similar among both Christians and pagans. Cicero (*De officiis* 1.11–13) had carefully distinguished two types of war: first, a defensive war, in which almost any means of resistance might be used, and second, a war fought to gain supremacy over a rival people. This kind of war could be undertaken only when provoked by some legitimating injustice, and it had to be pursued honorably, in a manner that would lay the foundation for lasting peace. Both types of war had as their objective, the establishment of a stable peace. Against this goal all else was to be measured.

In the first three historical phases, Christians seemed to regard the use of military force for the protection of the temporal order as a function proper to the government of the empire. Some served in the army, and most accounts of their witness to Christ neither conceal nor apologize for their military service. Others refused military service because they were concerned only with the heavenly kingdom, or because they saw the proper Christian contribution to the safety of the empire to be only through spiritual, not bodily means.

In the fourth phase, Eusebius undertook a theological justification of Constantine's war of conquest. The legitimating objective was a stable peace to be achieved by establishing a single ruler who would mirror the divine dominion over the universe. Ambrose, in the fifth phase, may have been thinking in the same vein when he praised Theodosius for overthrowing usurpers.

Only in Augustine do we find an explicit rejection of the Roman war of conquest, motivated as it was by a lust for domination. He seems to have approved of war only for defensive purposes and insisted that the motives of the individuals involved had to be love of neighbor. For example, in the private sphere, the use of force in self-defense was not allowed, because in that context the only motive that could be in play was self-love.

All in all, Christians seemed to have simply accepted warfare as a fact of life in a sinful world. Some exempted themselves from war and military service, but not from responsibility for its goals and objectives, as we saw in Origen. Others, in all five historical periods, seemed willing to enter military service in order to help resist the forces that threatened temporal peace.

The third theme: the superhuman or divine element in military power and warfare. Christian and pagan agreed in attributing success in warfare to a divine intervention. For the Romans, this meant that success in warfare meant the careful and regular cultivation of the gods. In the second and third historical phases, Christian objections to military service were largely based on the supposition that the power operative in the military was demonic. Only in the fourth and fifth phases did Christians assert that military action could be inspired and supported by God. This needs to be looked at more closely.

In the first phase, when Christians were a persecuted minority, we find two responses. On the one hand, the love command in the canonical New Testament calls Christians to free oppressors from the control of evil forces and win them over to Christ. In some of the canonical, and especially in the apocryphal materials, we find the desire for vindication evincing a similar judgment about the true source of persecution.

In the second phase, when Christians had become, at least to some extent, a tolerated minority, Christians were urged by Tertullian to keep out of the military because of the connection between military power and the cult of the demons in army religion. Origen taught that peace is promoted by spiritual power. Because Christians were no longer a distinct people, Origen did not expect God to intervene militarily to protect them as he had Israel.

But in the second and third phases, the witness also begins to become mixed. Apparently, many Christian soldiers and the officers under whom they served perceived no strict connection between the pagan religious cult and the valor and success of the soldiers. Christians stood on their service records, and judges attempted to rescue good troops from execution when they were accused on religious grounds.

In the fourth and fifth phases, Christian theologians continued to decry the working of demonic forces in warfare. But as Christians became a people more easily identifiable in the Roman Empire, some emperors could be recognized as champions raised up by God for the defense of his Church through their military campaigns. In the victories of Constantine, Christians begin to see God intervening to destroy the power of Satan. Now that Christians are beginning to be easily identified as a people, as a group within the empire, the Old Testament notion of a chosen people also begins to serve as an interpretative category.

In the fifth phase, Ambrose and Augustine begin to see the danger of the demonic forces at work also within the Christian rulers. They call these rulers to repent of vengeance or

excessive violence. Augustine saw God as promoting salvation
for the people not only by victory but even by defeat and
death. This analysis recognized a divine role in warfare, but
refused to place God at the service of his people's ambition or
desire for security.

Both the Christian and pagan theologians were convinced
that military victory involved more than human power. But, for
the Christians, the idea that God would get involved by using
military means against the demonic power, was a relatively late
development. It is found only in the fourth and fifth phases,
roughly from the time of Constantine.

Conclusion

Can any conclusions be drawn from all this? With regard
to each of these three themes—(1) attitudes toward human life
and culture, (2) ideas about the appropriate function of war,
(3) views on the superhuman or divine element in military
power and warfare—we find both continuity and difference
between the five different historical phases we outlined. *But,
in each phase, the Christian doctrine was shaped by the interaction of
faith in Christ and a particular sociopolitical setting. No Christian
attitudes toward the military, toward war, toward peace and the
search for peace, none of these Christian attitudes, even in the New
Testament itself, were independent of their cultural and sociopolitical
context.*

Our own age may seem quite discontinuous with that of
early Christianity. We have quite different values regarding
human life, the world of nature, and the cultural achievements
which are destroyed by war. That difference, plus the increasingly destructive power of war which can now destroy the human species and perhaps even our planet, makes war appear
less and less as an appropriate instrument for achieving peace
and security. And although we may not look upon them as demonic agents, we are indeed increasingly convinced of the role

of social evils, of passions or vices shared by whole peoples, as the sources of war and the destroyers of peace. The origin of war in sin is very evident to us, but we no longer so easily assume that God makes a divine use of military power to limit and overcome that evil.

Some Christians have recourse to the spiritual means Origen recommended, while others labor to implement the love command through political action, consciousness raising, laboring for social and economic reform, working for international agreements, and even by trying to make the deterrent of threatened mutual destruction work as an insurer of peace. Can all of these lay equal claim to be in continuity with the New Testament love command? The negative reply rises quickly to one's lips. But to give a well-grounded answer is, as we have tried to show, far more difficult. All that one can really be sure of is that there are no simple answers.

NOTES
. .

[1] Robert J. Daly, S.J., "The New Testament: Pacifism and Non-violence," *The American Ecclesiastical Review* 168 (1974):544–562; "The New Testament and Early Church," in J. T. Culliton, ed., *Non-violence—Central to Christian Spirituality: Perspectives from Scripture to the Present* Toronto Studies in Theology 8 (New York/Toronto: Edwin Mellen, 1982), pp. 34–62; *Christian Biblical Ethics. From Biblical Revelation to Contemporary Christian Praxis: Method and Content* (New York: Paulist Press, 1984), pp. 211–19; "Military Service and Early Christianity: A Methodological Approach," in E.A. Livingstone, ed., *Studia Patristica* 18:1.1–8; John Helgeland, Robert J. Daly and J. Patout Burns, *Christians and the Military: The Early Experience,* ed. R.J. Daly (Philadelphia: Fortress Press, 1985).

[2] E.g., see Roland Bainton, *Christian Attitudes Toward War and Peace* (Nashville/New York: Abingdon, 1960).

[3] René Coste, "Pacifism and Legitimate Defense," *Concilium* 5 (1965):87.

[4] My remarks here are especially indebted to Luise Schottroff, "Non-Violence and the Love of One's Enemies," in Luise Schottroff, et al., *Essays on the Love Command,* trans. R. H. and I. Fuller (Philadelphia: Fortress Press, 1978), pp. 9–39, and Pheme Perkins, *Love Commands in the New Testament* (New York: Paulist Press, 1982).

[5] *Christians and the Military,* p. 14.

[6] Ibid., pp. 14–15.

[7] Schottroff, p. 25.

[8] Ibid., pp. 15–16.

[9] These "five phases" and "three themes" follow the structure of the conclusion of *Christians and the Military,* pp. 87–93, but incorporate into that structure extensive material from the rest of the book.

[10] Ibid., p. 87.

[11] G. Dix and H. Chadwick, eds., *The Treatise on the Apostolic Tradition of St. Hippolytus of Rome* (London: SPCK, 1968), pp. 24–28.

[12] See Gerard E. Caspary, *Politics and Exegesis: Origen and the Two Swords* (Berkeley/London: University of California, 1979).

[13] See *The Martyrdom of Julius the Veteran* in Herbert Musurillo, *The Acts of the Christian Martyrs* (Oxford: Oxford University, 1972), pp. 260–65.

[14] See, e.g., *The Account of Thomas the Israelite Philosopher Concerning the Childhood of the Lord* in E. Hennecke and W. Schneemelcher, eds., ET and ed. R.McL. Wilson, *New Testament Apocrypha* (Philadelphia: Westminster, 1963) 1.392–393, 397.

[15] See G.F. Chesnut, *The First Christian Histories* (Paris: Gabriel Beauchesne, 1977), pp. 99–101.

[16] James Stevenson, *A New Eusebius: Documents Illustrative of the Church to A.D. 337* (London: SPCK, 1968), p. 322; C.J. Hefele, trans. J. Leclercq, *Histoire des Conciles* (Paris: Letourzey, 1907) 1.282.

[17] See esp. Augustine, *Letters* 189.2,4–7; 220.5–7 and *Against Faustus* 22.73–79.

Chapter Seven

INSPIRED AUTHORS AND SAINTLY INTERPRETERS IN CONFLICT: THE NEW TESTAMENT ON WAR AND PEACE

• • • • • •

David Whitten Smith

In questions of truly compelling human interest, important scriptural passages often give conflicting advice. So it is for questions of war and peace, violence and authority. Key values seem to be in conflict: justice cries out to be enforced, but force destroys peace. The dilemma is solved not by choosing one passage or one value and rejecting or ignoring the others, but by holding them in tension, allowing the divergent viewpoints to drive us to a deeper faith which will give us a new understanding and thus transform the problem.[1] This "new understanding" which "transforms the problem" may involve a personal conversion involving a change in our basic world view. For this reason, it is important to be aware of our world views and the images that express them, and conscious of how they may differ from those of the sacred or saintly authors we are reading.

This chapter studies three contrasting New Testament passages that are often used to support war or peace. With an historical study, we will consider how "saintly interpreters" holding different world views have attempted to bring meaning from apparent conflict between "inspired authors"—and

in the process have come into conflict among themselves. We
will consider the following three key passages:

Romans Chapter 13:

> Let every person be subordinate to the higher authori-
> ties, *for there is no authority except from God, and those that
> exist have been established by God. Therefore, whoever resists
> authority opposes what God has appointed,* and those who
> oppose it will bring judgment upon themselves. For rul-
> ers are not a cause of fear to good conduct, but to evil.
> Do you wish to have no fear of authority? Then do what
> is good and you will receive approval from it, for it is a
> servant of God for your good. But if you do evil, be
> afraid, *for it does not bear the sword without purpose; it is the
> servant of God to inflict wrath on the evildoer.* Therefore it
> is necessary to be subject not only because of the wrath
> but also because of conscience. [2]
>
> (Rom 13:1–5)

Revelation Chapter 13:

> Then I saw a beast come out of the sea with ten horns
> and seven heads; on its horns were ten diadems, and on
> its heads blasphemous name[s]. . . . *To it the dragon gave
> its own power and throne, along with great authority.* . . .
> Fascinated, the whole world followed after the beast.
> They worshipped the dragon because it gave its author-
> ity to the beast; they also worshipped the beast and
> said, "Who can compare with the beast or who can fight
> against it?" . . . [The beast] was also *allowed to wage war
> against the holy ones and conquer them, and it was granted
> authority over every tribe, people, tongue, and nation.* . . .
> Whoever has ears ought to hear these words.
> Anyone destined for captivity goes into captivity.

> Anyone destined to be slain by the sword shall be
> slain by the sword.
> *Such is the faithful endurance of the holy ones.*
>
> (Rev 13:1–4, 7, 9–11)

Matthew Chapter 5:

> "You have heard that it was said, 'An eye for an eye and
> a tooth for a tooth.' But I say to you, *offer no resistance to*
> *one who is evil.* When someone strikes you on [your]
> right cheek, turn the other one to him as well. . . .
>   "You have heard that it was said, 'You shall love
> your neighbor and hate your enemy.' But I say to you,
> *love your enemies, and pray for those who persecute you, that*
> *you may be children of your heavenly Father,* for he makes
> his sun rise on the bad and the good, and causes rain to
> fall on the just and the unjust.
>
> (Mt 5:38f, 43–45)

Rom 13:1–4[3] claims that *all authority* comes from *God* and
carries a sword, Revelation 13 (especially v. 2) claims that *the*
authority of the beast from the sea comes from *the dragon who is*
Satan (12:9) and who has been *allowed (by God) to conquer the*
faithful, and Mt 5:21–26, 38–48 (especially v. 39) calls on
Christians *not to resist evil.*[4] These passages stand most in tension if one interprets the beast of Revelation 13 as the Roman
empire (as most historical-critical commentators do) and if the
Sermon on the Mount is thought to speak to public as well as
private morality. Does political authority come from God or
from Satan? Should we obey authority to the point of wielding
the sword ourselves in defense of the state, should we refuse
to resist evil at all and thus accept oppression, should we use
active nonviolence of the sort that Gandhi practiced, or are
there other responsible interpretations?
    Interpreters through the centuries have dealt with these
apparent contradictions in a variety of ways, for example by ap-

plying Revelation to the Roman Catholic Church and Romans to the secular state, by claiming that Matthew refers to private morality and Romans to public morality, by claiming that Matthew is offering counsels of perfection for the perfect or for clergy alone, by claiming that Matthew is referring only to the end-times, or by choosing one passage and ignoring the others.

The historical study which follows is based on patristic, medieval, and reformation commentaries on Matthew, Romans, and the Apocalypse;[5] on references or allusions to our passages or to relevant points of theological vision (world view) in other primary literature (for example, in classical discussions of war and peace);[6] and on secondary literature.[7] For the earliest period I presuppose the study by Robert Daly in Chapter Six of this book, especially his reference to the "aggressively missionary attitude" of early Christians toward enemy and persecutor. Where I do refer to the same period, it is to consider different questions than he does. He gives considerable attention to early Christian attitudes on the legitimacy of war as such, while I am looking for early uses of our three passages in relation to authority, power, and violence in general.

I also consider it likely that the early centuries held and acted on visions that were imperfectly thought through and imperfectly related to each other. There is tension between the widespread refusal to act violently toward persecutors and the general acceptance of a world held together by the power of the Roman army. With the hindsight of almost twenty centuries, wisdom only implicit in the early centuries might become explicit and give rise to new judgments. Early centuries, like our own, included both grace and sin.

The Patristic Period

Tertullian (+ after 220)

Tertullian insisted that Christians must not act violently toward the persecuting state, noting that Christians must love

their enemies, may not retaliate to injury, and are "given am-
pler liberty to be killed than to kill." (*Apology* 37:1, 5)[8] He ap-
plies Matthew 5 even to Christian service in the secular state
when he argues that Christians cannot be soldiers.

> Shall the son of peace take part in the battle when it does
> not become him even to sue at law? And shall he apply the
> chain, and the prison, and the torture, and the punish-
> ment, who is not the avenger even of his own wrongs? (*The
> Chaplet* 11)[9]

He was willing to pray for the Roman empire because he believed that it was holding off the end-time woes (2 Thes 2:6).
While we are aware that Rome's collapse did not bring on the
end-times, some today may unconsciously feel that the collapse of Western democracy would be a tragedy of comparable
weight and that the United States is a God-given bulwark
against chaos:

> Without ceasing, for all our emperors we offer prayer. We
> pray for life prolonged; for security to the empire; for pro-
> tection to the imperial house; for brave armies, a faithful
> senate, a virtuous people, the world at rest, whatever, as
> man or Caesar, an emperor could wish. . . . For we know
> that a mighty shock impending over the whole earth—in
> fact, the very end of all things threatening dreadful woes—
> is only retarded by the continued existence of the Roman
> empire. We have no desire, then, to be overtaken by these
> dire events; and in praying that their coming may be de-
> layed, we are lending our aid to Rome's duration. (*Apology*
> 30:4 and 32:1)[10]

He also reflected Romans 13 when he claimed that Roman authority is God-given:

> We respect in the emperors the ordinance of God, who has
> set them over the nations. We know that there is that in
> them which God has willed; and to what God has willed
> we desire all safety. (*Apology* 32:3)[11]

In the Apocalypse Tertullian identified *Babylon* with Rome, but the *first beast* with the *antichrist*. Thus he avoided the most obvious tension between Romans and Revelation, yet he was ambiguous about Roman glory:

> Is the laurel of triumph made of leaves, or of corpses? Is it adorned with ribbons, or with tombs? Is it bedewed with ointments, or with the tears of wives and mothers? It may be of some Christians too, for Christ is also among the barbarians. (*The Chaplet* 12)[12]

It seems to be the pagans' demand that Christians swear by the "genius" of the emperor that moved Tertullian to mention Christian exorcism and its role in promoting the public weal. This matter-of-fact reference to exorcism is foreign to the world view of many Christians today:

> Though we decline to swear by the genii of the Caesars, we swear by their safety, which is worth far more than all your genii. . . . But as for daemons, that is your genii, we have been in the habit of exorcising them, not of swearing by them. . . . Who would save you . . . from the attacks of those spirits of evil, which without reward or hire we exorcise? (*Apology* 32:2f and 37:9)[13]

Ambrose of Milan (c. 339–397)

Ambrose reflects the new alliance between state and Church. He was a Roman governor before becoming bishop of Milan. His writings and actions reflect the questions raised by Revelation and Romans. Ambrose supported just war to defend the state. Nevertheless he was willing to resist state power when he believed that it was being misused. In two cases in particular, he exercised an active nonviolence that sounds surprisingly modern. When the emperor's mother ordered Ambrose to deliver over a certain church to be used for Arian worship, Ambrose and a crowd of Christians staged a stand-in. Gothic troops surrounded the church, but at the last minute the courtiers refused to order an attack. Ambrose is reported to have said:

> We priests have our own ways of rising to Empire. Our infirmity is our way to the throne. For *When I am weak, then am I powerful.*[14]

When the emperor Theodosius needlessly slaughtered thousands in his siege of Thessalonica, Ambrose refused to celebrate Eucharist in the emperor's presence, then wrote a letter to the emperor explaining his actions. The letter is respectful. It calls on the emperor to repent publicly. One sentence in the letter relates to Romans 13, stating well how Christians should pray for their government:

> We should entreat [God] to take away all disturbances, to preserve peace for you emperors, that the faith and peace of the Church, whose advantage it is that emperors should be Christians and devout, may continue.[15]

Yet we see from the tenor of the whole letter how far Ambrose was from offering blind obedience to the emperor.

John Chrysostom (?354–407)

Chrysostom spent the early part of his life as an ascetic and the latter part preaching to the rich, so he is well placed to tell us whether the Sermon on the Mount distinguishes precept from counsel. In fact, he makes a point to bring the two ways of life together, denying that those "in the world" are any less called to perfection, with the single exception of celibacy.[16]

In 387 Antioch rioted against new taxes, publicly mocking and insulting images of the emperor. After their drunken demonstration they realized the gravity of their act—too late. Massive arrests, torture and executions followed. The city was terrorized. In this somber atmosphere, Chrysostom reminded the people that they were pilgrims on this earth and must expect to suffer. Life and fortune should not be central to us. He also reminded his hearers that even those who were innocent of the rioting, many of whom were caught in the net of terror, still were implicated in the situation, because they had failed to confront the blasphemers and Godless who were primarily responsible, with the demands of the Gospel.[17]

Meanwhile another witness to Christian disdain of life and fortune was developing. Word of the tragedy reached monks and hermits round about Antioch. They came down into the city and offered their own lives to the imperial authorities in atonement for the guilty. They refused to go away until either the people received pardon or they were sent along with the guilty for punishment. They also reminded the magistrates of their responsibility if they condemned and executed the innocent. This confrontative active nonviolence astonished the judges and was an important factor in the eventual pardon. Under pressure of the terror, the churches filled. People seemed repentant. But Chrysostom was not impressed. And after the danger had passed, everything returned to selfish normalcy.

Chrysostom insisted that the demands of the Sermon on the Mount are not mere hyperbole.[18] They do not promise that we will escape suffering by keeping them.[19] In fact, commenting on Mt 5:39, he states that we do confront evil but not in the world's way. We resist evil by surrendering ourselves to undeserved suffering. In this way we call the oppressor to conversion through shame. We need not fear that such action is "impractical" because either no one would attack people of such attitude, or if one did and we gave away all our clothes, our neighbors would clothe us; or if no one did our very nakedness would be an honor. (One thinks of the famous scene where Francis of Assisi returned his clothes to his father on demand. In that case it was the bishop who clothed him.)[20] By such action we free those bound by hate and become like God in forgiveness.[21]

With the mention of the court in Mt 5:25 Chrysostom re-

lates Rom 13:4 and the sword of government, suggesting that
Paul is speaking for those who are still too attached to the
world, while those who truly follow the Sermon would not
need to be reminded of such a punishment.[22] Finally Chrysostom notes that wars are the plaything of the rich, not of the
poor.[23] We will see Chrysostom's view of the world, his de-
valuation of power and riches and emphasis on spiritual realities, reflected again in the teaching of Augustine. These
attitudes challenge many of the presuppositions on which our
quest for "security" is based.

Augustine of Hippo (354–430)

Augustine is such a key thinker, both for theology in general and for war in particular, that a more detailed treatment of
his thought is important.

Augustine's World View

For Augustine, sin is a pervasive reality, present from before birth and hidden within the depths of our being. It persists
in our actions even after we will to eliminate it.[24] We can never
know for sure to what extent our whole self agrees with our
conscious self.[25]

God and spirits are active in the world of our experience.
Augustine denied the common pagan belief that demons are
necessary go-betweens linking humans to the gods,[26] but he
asserted that they incite persecutors against Christians and can
be exorcised.[27] God controls all human events including government actions and wars, distributing peace, domination, and
submission according to his mysterious judgment. He is responsible even for the domination of evil rulers.[28]

Sin leads humans to deny guilt and to rely on themselves.
But they can be saved only if they admit their guilt and rely
on God, submitting to a therapy beyond their control.[29] Force
and punishment are useful and Christian if they are motivated
by love. Augustine used this principle to justify the forced con-

version of Donatists and pagans. He felt that the "inconveniences" caused by force could place people in a situation where they would be more open to conversion and growth.[30] The purpose of human life is dominated by eternal values. Earthly goods are true goods, but they are secondary to eternal ones, they are only "solace to our misery."[31] We should hold cheap those blessings and good things which are shared by good and evil humans alike, valuing those eternal goods that are reserved for the good alone.[32]

Rome was sacked because its inhabitants wanted to defend unjust affluence and freedom to sin.[33] Rome seemed to be heroic, but it was really lusting after glory.[34] Christians are responsible to call others to conversion. If they fail in this responsibility, they reveal that they don't truly love their enemies and that they love this world too much—they hold back for fear of rejection or persecution. Christians as well as pagans suffered at the sack of Rome because, although Christians were not guilty of pagan vices, they were guilty of failing to confront the pagans and rescue them from their vices.[35] There is no earthly security or absolute defense. God alone is in control, by his inscrutable providence. He can bring good even out of evil. Nevertheless, just war is allowed in some circumstances.[36]

Augustine and the Sermon on the Mount

In his commentary on Matthew's Gospel, Augustine discusses the Sermon on the Mount at length. He illustrates a number of principles important to interpretation,[37] some of which are disputed.

He emphasizes that it is attitudes, not mere acts, which are most important. On turning the other cheek, he says we should not boast but be ready in the heart to do so. He may well be thinking of the Donatists who acknowledged as Christian only the perfect. Yet his discussion makes it clear that he intends to include real actions, not just inner attitudes alone. This is clear from his concern whether perhaps slaves should be excluded from those things we are willing to give up in court, on the grounds that we are dealing here with people, not things, and Christians should not easily give up the influence for good they can have on bringing their slaves to the faith.[38]

Similarly, Augustine emphasizes that we offer not only the other *cheek* but also our *love* to the striker. Drawing this out with reference to other Scripture passages, he notes that when Jesus was struck on the cheek at his trial, rather than responding in a rigid compliance with this saying by turning the other cheek, he confronted his assailants with the truth by challenging their action. Yet his attitude was in agreement with this saying, since he offered his whole body to further blows.[39] This observation corresponds well with modern principles of nonviolent action where the point is to remain vulnerable rather than injure the enemy, yet to love them enough to confront them with truth despite their power to hurt us.

In discussing "an eye for an eye" Augustine draws out a certain progress: first, not to do evil which would merit punishment; then, if one suffers evil, to return no more than the evil received even though the guilty one deserves more than he causes; then not to retaliate at all; finally even to bless the persecutor.[40] One senses a concern to begin with his people where they are, not to crush them with excessive demands, but gradually to draw them on further. This approach is consonant with his Catholic (as opposed to Donatist) sense that he should minister to the weak as well as to the strong. It is also reflected in the extensive medieval development of the distinction between precepts and counsels of perfection.

Introducing implicit conditions, he understands "give to those who ask" to mean "give—but not necessarily what they ask for." If one should harm neither self nor other, one should refuse to give hurtful things. Give correction to those who ask for something unjust.[41] Becoming more controversial, he claims that punishment given lovingly is compatible with these passages. Punishment to correct is merciful, but only if the one punishing has overcome all hatred. Further, the punisher leaves himself or herself open to receive more injury. Augustine allows even capital punishment, since death is not the evil most think it is, yet because people think it is it can put the fear of God into them. Even if those killed are impenitent, at least they will be cut off before they can make their eternity even worse by more sin. Despite this general principle, Augustine opposed the execution of Donatists because it cut off the possibility of their conversion.[42]

Augustine on the Apocalypse

Augustine understood the millennium symbolically of the time of the Church from Jesus to the end of time. Within that period there are two "cities" which hold sway in the world: the city of God and the city of the devil. The first beast of Revelation 13 represents the city of the devil which includes both unbelievers and evil Christians. The New Jerusalem is already in the world: it is the city of God. Faithful Christians are part of the city of God, but they cannot avoid relationship with the city of the devil: this is the tragedy of our situation. Augustine's sense of sin and how deeply it is rooted in the world we inhabit gives his writing a special character.[43]

Augustine on War and Peace

Augustine defends Old Testament narratives of holy war against the Manichean Faustus. Manicheans rejected the Old Testament in part because they claimed that war is unworthy of God. In response, Augustine distinguishes between an act, its agent, and the authority under which the agent acts. Death is not the evil humans think it is; therefore the agent is praised or blamed depending on whether he was properly authorized. God has authority to order war or death, as does competent state authority.

> What is the evil in war? Is it the death of some who will soon die in any case, that others may live in peaceful subjection? This is mere cowardly dislike, not any religious feeling. The real evils in war are love of violence, revengeful cruelty, fierce and implacable enmity, wild resistance,

> and the lust of power, and such like; and it is generally to
> punish these things, when force is required to inflict the
> punishment, that, in obedience to God or some lawful au-
> thority, good men undertake wars.[44]

In this same letter Augustine confronts the objection that we
are ordered to turn the other cheek. He repeats his comment
that this passage enjoins an attitude of heart, not a bodily action.[45] In this case his argument is less secure. It is dangerous
to use the Old Testament to explain a New Testament saying
that is *explicitly* in antithesis to "what was said to the ancients."

Note that Augustine's arguments are conditioned by his
desire to uphold the Old Testament. In *The City of God* he adds
in effect: Be sure it really is God who is ordering it! Morton
Kelsey notes that both John Wilkes Booth (Abraham Lincoln's
assassin) and Lee Harvey Oswald (John Kennedy's assassin)
were themselves killed by men (Boston Corbett and Jack
Ruby) who claimed they had been deputed by God for the
task. This is one of the points where modern visions can find
room for the "demonic"—as a destructive unconscious "au-
tonomous complex" leading humans to see their power play as
a divine crusade. National leaders are as vulnerable to such a
spirit as are neurotic assassins.[46]

Another document often quoted to illustrate Augustine's
attitude toward war is his letter to Count Boniface. The general's wife had died and he wrote asking Augustine whether he
should retire to a monastery. Augustine urged him to maintain
his commission. This letter is often interpreted in the light of
the threatening barbarian invasions, but in fact at the time Augustine was more concerned with suppressing the Donatists
and with defending Africa from traditional nomads to the
south. As it turns out, Boniface was an ambitious career man—
he was not about to be pinned down on the desert border of
Africa. Within a few years Augustine saw Boniface court the
emperor for favor, marry a rich Arian wife, pick up a few con-
solation concubines, and settle down to defend Carthage
against *Rome*, ignoring the mounting barbarian threat. About

ten years after his first letter, Augustine wrote another tacitly but carefully withdrawing his support. By the time the real barbarians came, Augustine had no military heroes to rely on.[47]

Because he had a tragic sense of the world we live in, Augustine could combine a sense of the injustice of the Roman empire with support for its role in maintaining order and justice. He supported both just war *and just torture* (for the second of which he is rarely quoted today) but set strict limits for war and recognized that the necessity for both is tragic.

He considered at length the plight of the judge who must use torture to seek the truth, knowing that as a result he will torture some innocent people and perhaps condemn them because they were moved by the torture to confess to crimes they did not commit, and he will release some guilty and condemn their accusers because they were able to withstand the torture despite their guilt. At the end it is hard to see how useful torture could be to determine guilt.

As to Roman wars, he recognized their value in providing unity, yet wondered whether that unity is worth the cost in suffering:

> How many great wars, how much slaughter and bloodshed, have provided this unity! And though these are past, the end of these miseries has not yet come. For though there have never been wanting, nor are yet wanting, hostile nations beyond the empire, against whom wars have been and are waged, yet, supposing that there were no such nations, the very extent of the empire itself has produced wars of a more obnoxious description—social and civil wars (*The City of God* 19.7).[48]

Commenting on both torture and war, he emphasized the misery of a life that makes them necessary:

> Though we therefore acquit the judge of malice, we must none the less condemn human life as miserable (Ibid. 19:6).

> But, say they, the wise man will wage just wars. As if he would not all the rather lament the necessity of just wars,

if he remembers that he is a man. . . . Let everyone,
then, who thinks with pain on all these great evils, so
horrible, so ruthless, acknowledge that this is misery.
And if any one either endures or thinks of them without
mental pain, this is a more miserable plight still, for he
thinks himself happy because he has lost human feeling
(Ibid. 19:7).

Comparing human body and soul with the two cities, he
pointed out that only a soul which knows and is subject to the
true God can be a fitting mistress of the body. This is another
point at which demonic influence is mentioned:

What kind of mistress of the body and the vices can that
mind be which is ignorant of the true God, and which, instead of being subject to His authority, is prostituted to
the corrupting influences of the most vicious demons?
(Ibid. 19:25)

Similarly only a people in right relation with the true God can
properly manage the city, yet the citizens of the city of God
benefit from the so-called peace of the city of the devil which
he here identifies with Babylon. Note the allusions to 1 Peter,
the relation to our passages Romans 13 and Revelation 13, and
the reference to Jeremiah counseling the Jews in exile to pray
for *Babylon*, indicating that, in his view, "Pauline" obedience
is not based on the Christian, Jewish, or virtuous nature of the
authority obeyed—communist authorities have the same claim
to obedience.

Wherefore, as the life of the flesh is the soul, so the
blessed life of man is God, of whom the sacred writings of
the Hebrews say, "Blessed is the people whose God is the
Lord." Miserable, therefore, is the people which is alienated from God. Yet even this people has a peace of its own
which is not to be lightly esteemed, though, indeed, it
shall not in the end enjoy it, because it makes no good use
of it before the end. But it is in our interest that it enjoy
this peace meanwhile in this life; for as long as the two

cities are commingled, we also enjoy the peace of Babylon. For from Babylon the people of God is so freed that
it meanwhile sojourns in its company. And therefore the
apostle also admonished the Church to pray for kings and
those in authority, assigning as the reason, "that we may
live a quiet and tranquil life in all godliness and love." And
the prophet Jeremiah, when predicting the captivity that
was to befall the ancient people of God, and giving them
the divine command to go obediently to Babylonia, and
thus serve their God, counselled them also to pray for
Babylonia, saying, "In the peace thereof shall ye have
peace"—the temporal peace which the good and the
wicked together enjoy (Ibid. 19:26).

Along with this pervasive sense of tragedy, Augustine insisted
that just war must be carried on with love for the enemy.[49]

It is interesting that these two aspects so central to Augustine's treatment of just war, a tragic sense and love of the
enemy, seem often to have been lost by those who appeal to
him in support of just war despite their attention to the specific
criteria he proposed for just war.

Augustine's treatment of just war was influenced by the
dangers of the time in which he lived. Heretical movements
threatened the Church and barbarians threatened the Roman
empire. Although this is an oversimplification, we often picture his theory as making the defense of that empire possible
and preventing the unimaginable tragedy of its destruction. In
fact, the armed defense was unsuccessful: the barbarians did
destroy the empire. The just war did not succeed in its purpose: the "unimaginable" happened. While that destruction
had serious effects on civilization, it did not mean the end of
Christianity. The barbarians brought their own martial attitudes which were only gradually mitigated through the efforts
of the medieval Church: the Roman Church had given them
little reason to question those attitudes. It is interesting to
speculate what might have happened if the Roman world had
responded to the barbarian invasions with loving active non-

violence, challenging their martial attitudes with an alternative and effective response.[50]

It might be objected that the people did not have the commitment necessary to make such a nonviolent program work. But in fact they did not have the unselfish commitment to make an armed resistance possible, either. When desire for ease and selfish advantage dominate, arms aren't much help: they can wear themselves out in domestic squabbles without ever effectively engaging the foreign enemy.

The Early Middle Ages

Thomas Aquinas (1225–1274)

Aquinas supported government because it is instituted to promote the common good and order. He accepted just war in support of duly constituted government, but included among his conditions for just war the requirement that it be declared by the head of the legitimate government.[51] At the same time, he accepted rebellion in cases of true tyranny when the ruler does not promote the common good but rather his own individual good at the expense of the common good. In these cases he did not consider the government to be legitimate because it was not fulfilling the function of government. He went so far as to say that in these cases it is the king who is in rebellion.[52] His position in this respect is in contrast to that of Luther (see below).

Thomas did not write a commentary on the Apocalypse, but he faced our problem of passages in tension squarely when he laid out his conditions for just war. His basic conditions are that the war be declared by competent authority, that it be for just cause (deserved because of a fault for which one refuses to make restoration or amends), and that the intention be right (restore peace, punish evil, support good).[53] In his discussion he deals with both Mt 5:39 (and parallel in Rom 12:19) and with Rom 13:4.

For the first two, he explains that we should be *ready* to obey the command, although there are times when it should not be obeyed because of the common good or the good of our opponent:

> Such like precepts . . . should always be borne in readiness of mind, so that we be ready to obey them, and, if necessary, to refrain from resistance or self-defense. Nevertheless it is necessary sometimes for a man to act otherwise for the common good, or for the good of those with whom he is fighting. Hence Augustine says . . . "Those whom we have to punish with a kindly severity, it is necessary to handle in many ways against their will. For when we are stripping a man of the lawlessness of sin, it is good for him to be vanquished, since nothing is more hopeless than the happiness of sinners, whence arises a guilty impunity, and an evil will, like an internal enemy."[54]

He argues from Rom 13:4, interpreting "the sword" to refer to police action against internal enemies and arguing that by analogy competent authority can war against external enemies for the common good. But he insists that only competent authority has the right to the sword, except for the case of resistance to tyranny as mentioned above.[55] Notice that in the exception Thomas made to nonresistance, his motive included the good of the opponent who needs to be rescued from sin. Such a goal is more readily achieved by an active nonviolence that confronts opponents without killing them. Corpses vaporized by a nuclear explosion cannot repent.

Thomas also deals with war when he answers objections to Old Testament laws.[56] Here he demands that the government have just cause, offer peace to the opponent, and act with moderation. *Herem* (the total destruction of an opponent) was only by express command of God and as punishment for sin. Thomas did not allow clerics and bishops to take part personally in even just wars, except to encourage the laity through their prayers and preaching. War is a distraction from prayer

and contemplation, and clerics should imitate the self-sacrific-
ing love of Jesus whose sacrament they celebrate.[57] Some today ask whether it is only the clergy whose relation to the
sacrament excludes war.

The Reformation

Martin Luther (1483–1546)

In this treatment I am reflecting primarily on four of Luther's writings: *Temporal Authority*, his commentary on the Sermon on the Mount, *Lectures on Romans*, and *Whether Soldiers
Too Can Be Saved*.

In *Temporal Authority*, Luther taught that true Christians
do not need law, since they do good and avoid evil whether
there is a law about it or not. But there must be law for non-
Christians to avoid chaos in society, and Christians who love
their non-Christian neighbors can show that love by enforcing
the law on their behalf. Luther then interpreted the prohibition of violence in the Sermon on the Mount in these terms:
Christians must not sue at law or use political, police, or military force for their own benefit; but they can and should do so
for the good of their non-Christian neighbors:

> No Christian shall wield or invoke the sword for himself
> and his cause. In behalf of another, however, he may and
> should wield it and invoke it to restrain wickedness and to
> defend godliness.[58]

> If you see that there is a lack of hangmen, constables,
> judges, lords, or princes, and you find that you are quali-
> fied, you should offer your services and seek the position,
> that the essential governmental authority may not be des-
> pised and become enfeebled or perish. The world cannot
> and dare not dispense with it.[59]

In his commentary on the Sermon on the Mount, Luther made
a basic distinction between the earthly kingdom symbolized
by God's left hand, ruled by God through secular authority,

and the spiritual kingdom symbolized by his right hand, ruled
through his word. Luther attacked Catholics for confusing the
two by assigning secular authority to the Church, and Anabap-
tists for confusing the two by trying to rule the secular sphere
through the ten commandments and the Sermon on the
Mount.[60]

Luther taught that the two kingdoms must be kept distinct in theory although they were united in an individual human. As a person each Christian is subject only to God, but as
to their bodies and outward goods Christians are subject to secular authority. As Luther explains it, the specifically Christian
seems to be confined to the heart while one's actions are determined by secular norms:

> Thus when a Christian goes to war or when he sits on a
> judge's bench, punishing his neighbor, or when he regis-
> ters an official complaint, he is not doing this as a Chris-
> tian, but as a soldier or a judge or a lawyer. At the same
> time he keeps a Christian heart. He does not intend any-
> one any harm, and it grieves him that his neighbor must
> suffer grief.[61]

Christians are counseled just to leave secular affairs to secular
authority without applying Christian norms to them:

> Do you want to know what your duty is as a prince or a
> judge or a lord or a lady, with people under you? You do
> not have to ask Christ about your duty. Ask the imperial
> or the territorial law.[62]

As a result, Jesus' sayings seem to apply to our outward acts
only when we are *forced* to observe them:

> [Jesus] is not tampering with the responsibility and au-
> thority of the government, but He is teaching His individ-
> ual Christians how to live personally, apart from their
> official position and authority. They should not desire re-
> venge at all. They should have the attitude that if some-
> one hits them on one cheek, they are ready, *if need be*, to
> turn the other cheek to him as well.[63]

> If someone takes your coat, you shall not seek revenge. Rather, *if there is nothing you can do to prevent it,* you shall let him take your cloak as well.[64]

> As individual persons we have no power or defense against the government if it should set itself against us. But where this is not the case and you can use the law to defend and protect yourself against some violence to you or yours, then it is your right *and your duty* to do so.[65]

These passages differ from the attitude he expressed in *Temporal Authority*, where Christians were *not* to defend *themselves.*

Luther states that *we individually* must love God's enemies at the same time as we remain enemies to them, that is, refuse to join them in their opposition to God. But *public authority* must "hate"—that is, combat—God's enemies.[66] In his lectures on Romans, Luther urges this same distinction between the two kingdoms. He scolds the Catholic Church for having taken over the secular realm and engages in a long and juicy diatribe against bishops. He apologizes for it, saying he only does so because his office of preacher demands it. Significantly, he says, "I am not sure, but I am inclined to think that the secular powers fulfill their office better and more happily than the ecclesiastical ones do."[67] With regard to obedience to secular authorities, a marginal gloss argues that Christians must submit even to non-Christian and evil rulers, because the office and its powers are from God even if the holder of the office is evil.[68]

In 1522 Luther thought that the Apocalypse was not authentic prophecy. When he was introduced to the anti-papal interpretation, he began to esteem its prophecy more highly. He produced an edition of Purvaeus' commentary in 1528, writing a new introduction for it. Later in the introduction to his New Testament (1534) he commented again briefly on Revelation. For Luther, the two beasts of chapter 13 are the empire and the papacy. The papacy, through Charlemagne, healed the wound that had killed the pagan empire. Many Protestants followed his interpretation.[69]

Few scholars today would agree with Luther that it was John's intention to identify the beast from the sea with the Roman Catholic Church. But this identification contains an element of truth. If every government or human institution includes an aspect of sin and a tendency to self-glorification, the Catholic Church cannot claim to be exempt, especially in those periods in which it exercises considerable secular political power. Insofar as that sinful aspect becomes realized, the Catholic Church shows the face of the first beast, and those individuals and institutions that support and justify those sinful aspects of the Church reflect the image of the second beast. But the reformers should have applied these same principles to the new churches they were founding and to the princes who were providing them with support. All human institutions and governments come under God's judgment.

Luther applied Romans 13 to civil rulers, believing that they were more trustworthy than the Church rulers he was battling. His distinction of authority into two kingdoms allowed him to urge obedience to civil authorities despite their sin and to counsel disobedience to ecclesiastical authority because of its sin and faithlessness. In contrast to Augustine's distinction of two cities—a distinction that was based on faithfulness or sin and that cut through both civil and ecclesiastical government—Luther's distinction was simply between civil and ecclesiastical spheres of action. In his work *Whether Soldiers Too Can Be Saved* he uses Romans 13 so frequently and so consistently that he loses Augustine's sense of tragedy and almost seems to glory in war:

> The very fact that the sword has been instituted by God to punish the evil, protect the good, and preserve peace is powerful and sufficient proof that war and killing along with all the things that accompany wartime and martial law have been instituted by God. . . . When I think of a soldier fulfilling his office by punishing the wicked, killing the wicked, and creating so much misery, it seems an unChristian work completely contrary to Christian love. But

when I think of how it protects the good and keeps and
preserves wife and child, house and farm, property, and
honor and peace, then I see how precious and godly this
work is. . . . The hand that wields this sword and kills
with it is not man's hand, but God's; and it is not
man, but God, who hangs, tortures, beheads, kills, and
fights. . . .[70]

[Christian soldiers] should be exhorted like this, "Dear
comrades, we are gathered here to serve, obey, and do our
duty to our prince, for according to God's will and ordi-
nance we are bound to support our prince with our body
and our possessions, even though in God's sight we are as
poor sinners as our enemies are. Nevertheless, since we
know that our prince is in the right in this case, or at least
do not know otherwise, we are therefore sure and certain
that in serving and obeying him we are serving God. Let
everyone, then, be brave and courageous and let no one
think otherwise than that his fist is God's fist, his spear
God's spear, and cry with heart and voice, 'For God and
the emperor!' If God gives us victory, the honor and praise
shall be his, not ours, for he wins it through us poor sinners. But we will take the booty and the wages as presents
and gifts of God's goodness and grace to us, though we are
unworthy, and sincerely thank him for them. Now God
grant the victory! Forward with joy."[71]

It should be noted that Luther makes exception for the case
of unjust war. If a prince chooses to fight an unjust war, the
Christian warrior is bound to refuse to take part.[72] But the
weight of the argument is so strongly in favor of cooperation
that readers can be excused for missing this point. For example, in Nazi Germany, the weight of Church advice was in favor of fighting to protect the nation despite doubts about the
justice of the war itself.

With regard to rebellion, Luther teaches that Christians
are not allowed to rebel; they must patiently suffer under their
ruler. If they rebel, they should be punished by the ruler.[73]

Luther blames those who start a war, claiming that a

prince should go to war only if the war has been forced on him. This is quite a different principle from that of Thomas Aquinas, who bases the justification for war not on the question who started it but on the question whether the war promotes justice.[74] A leader may go to war to restore something which has been unjustly seized or to redress an injustice which the opponent is unwilling to make good.

John Calvin (1509–1564)

Calvin referred to Romans 13 to insist that subjects are not to revolt against even a tyrant. The authority of even a tyrant comes from God, and fulfills his purpose by punishing the guilty and testing the innocent. Calvin admitted that sometimes God raises up someone to punish the tyrant. But he did not allow that the one raised up be one of the tyrant's Christian subjects. The one exception he allowed to the authority of unjust leaders was that Christians must not obey when leaders draw them away from obedience to God.[75] Neither Luther nor Calvin followed Thomas' position that a tyrant seeking his own selfish good rather than the common good is exercising authority illegitimately and may be justly resisted.

Conclusions

The limitations of this format do not allow me to present fully my own interpretation, but a final summary of viewpoints implicit in the preceding discussion should clarify the purposes of this chapter.[76] Chrysostom and Augustine's world views challenge our views of what we need to protect and open the way to a fearless active nonviolence that seeks to convert the enemy. Augustine's view of the two cities that cut across all human institutions warns us not to absolutize either Church or nation and offers the understanding of Romans and Revelation as reflecting two aspects of all human institutions: the "vocation" that human institutions and structures have to promote good and restrain evil is from God, while the distortion and subversion of that vocation in favor of the personal advantage and privilege of those in authority is from Satan.[77] The tendency to see one's own group as acting on behalf of God's authority and the opposing group as acting in the power of Satan is a "demonic" temptation of great power that promotes destructive crusades. An active nonviolent response holds the promise, in God's grace, of denying that demonic crusade the legitimacy it seeks.[78]

NOTES
· ·

¹ See Paul Tournier, *To Resist or To Surrender*, trans. John S. Gilmour (Atlanta: John Knox Press, 1964), especially pp. 56–64.

² The translation for these three passages is from the Revised New Testament of the New American Bible, copyright 1986 by the Confraternity of Christian Doctrine, Washington, D.C. Emphases added.

³ 1 Pet 2:13–25 is similar.

⁴ Matthew is also in tension with *Old Testament* accounts of holy war, but in context Matthew 5 is explicitly a "fulfillment" of the Old Testament and as such it includes significant change from Old Testament practices and judgments. There is of course much dispute about what Matthew means by "fulfill." Not all would agree that it implies change from the Old Testament. See Harvey K. McArthur, "The Sermon and the Mosaic Tradition," in *Understanding the Sermon on the Mount* (New York: Harper & Brothers, 1960), pp. 26–57.

⁵ For the Sermon on the Mount, the most helpful bibliography of commentaries with a discussion of the history of interpretation is found in Warren S. Kissinger, *The Sermon on the Mount: A History of Interpretation and Bibliography*, ATLA Bibliography Series, no. 3 (Metuchen, NJ: Scarecrow and the American Theological Library Association, 1975). For the Apocalypse of John see E. B. Allo, "Les commentateurs de l'Apocalypse," in *Saint Jean l'Apocalypse*, Etudes Bibliques (Paris: J. Gabalda, Librairie Victor Lecoffre, 1921), pp. ccxvi–ccxl; and Isbon T. Beckwith, *The Apocalypse of John: Studies in Introduction with a Critical and Exegetical Commentary* (1919; reprint, Grand Rapids, Mich.: Baker Book House, 1979).

⁶ A very useful collection of texts is Arthur F. Holmes, ed., *War and Christian Ethics* (Grand Rapids, Mich.: Baker Book House, Cannon, 1975). Other texts for the early period are found with extensive discussion in Louis J. Swift, *The Early Fathers on War and Military Service*, Message of the Fathers of the Church 19 (Wilmington: Michael Glazier, 1983) and in John Helgeland et al.,

Christians and the Military: The Early Experience, ed. Robert J. Daly (Philadelphia: Fortress Press, 1985).

[7] Useful general studies of Christian attitudes toward war and government are Adolf Harnack, *Militia Christi: The Christian Religion and the Military in the First Three Centuries,* trans. David McInnes Gracie (Philadelphia: Fortress Press, 1981; original German edition 1905); Cecil John Cadoux, *The Early Church and the World: A History of the Christian Attitude to Pagan Society and the State Down to the Time of Constantinus* (Edinburgh: T. & T. Clark, 1925) and *The Early Christian Attitude to War* (New York: Seabury, Vineyard, 1982); Roland H. Bainton, *Christian Attitudes Toward War and Peace: A Historical Survey and Critical Re-evaluation* (Nashville: Abingdon, 1960); Frederick H. Russell, *The Just War in the Middle Ages,* Cambridge Studies in Medieval Life and Thought, third series, vol. 8 (London: Cambridge University Press, 1975); Jean-Michel Hornus, *It Is Not Lawful For Me To Fight: Early Christian Attitudes Toward War, Violence, and the State,* rev. ed., trans. Alan Kreider and Oliver Coburn (Scottdale, Pa.: Herald Press, Christian peace shelf, 1980); John Helgeland, "Christians and the Roman Army from Marcus Aurelius to Constantine" in *Aufstieg und Niedergang der Römischen Welt: Geschichte und Kultur Roms im Spiegel der Neuren Forschung,* II Principat, 23:1, Herausgegeben von Wolfgang Haase (Berlin: Walter de Gruyter, 1979), pp. 724–834; John Helgeland, Robert J. Daly and J. Patout Burns, *Christians and the Military: The Early Experience,* ed. R. J. Daly (Philadelphia: Fortress Press, 1985); and Ronald G. Musto, *The Catholic Peace Tradition* (Maryknoll, N.Y.: Orbis Books, 1986).

[8] Tertullian, *Apology,* Loeb Classical Library, trans. T. R. Glover (Cambridge, MA: Harvard University Press, 1966).

[9] Tertullian, *The Chaplet* or *De Corona,* pp. 93–103 in A. Cleveland Coxe, ed., American Edition, *Latin Christianity: Its Founder, Tertullian,* vol. 3 of *The Ante-Nicene Fathers: Translations of the Writings of the Fathers down to A.D. 325,* ed. Alexander Roberts and James Donaldson, rev. A. Cleveland Coxe (Buffalo: The Christian Literature Publishing Company, 1885; reprint, Grand Rapids: Eerdmans, 1980), p. 99.

[10] Tertullian, *Apology,* trans. S. Thelwall, pp. 17–55 in *Ante-Nicene Fathers* vol. 3 (note 9 above), pp. 42–43.

[11] Ibid., p. 43.

[12] Tertullian, *The Chaplet,* p. 101.

¹³ Tertullian, *Apology*, tr. S. Thelwall, pp. 43 and 45.
¹⁴ Quoted in Peter Brown, *Augustine of Hippo: A Biography* (Berkeley: University of California Press, 1969), p. 82; see also pp. 81 and 103.
¹⁵ Ambrose, "Letter 51," pp. 450–453 in *Some of the Principal Works of St. Ambrose*, trans. H. De Romestin, vol. 10 of *A Select Library of Nicene and Post-Nicene Fathers of the Christian Church*, second series, ed. Philip Schaff and Henry Wace (New York: The Christian Literature Company, 1896; reprint, Grand Rapids: Eerdmans, 1979) par. 14 p. 452.
¹⁶ Chrysostomos Baur, O.S.B., *John Chrysostom and His Time*, trans. Sr. M. Gonzaga, R.S.M., two volumes (Westminster, Md.: Newman, 1959) 1:111.
¹⁷ Ibid., vol. 1 chapter 22. Note especially page 265.
¹⁸ John Chrysostom, *The Preaching of Chrysostom: Homilies on the Sermon on the Mount*, The Preacher's Paperback Library, ed. Jaroslav Pelikan (Philadelphia: Fortress Press, 1967) 16.5 (hom. 16 par. 5, pp. 10f).
¹⁹ Ibid. 15.8.
²⁰ Ibid. 18.1–3.
²¹ Ibid. 18.5–7.
²² Ibid. 16.13.
²³ Ibid. 15.15.
²⁴ Peter Brown, *Augustine of Hippo* (note 14 above), pp. 148ff.
²⁵ Ibid., p. 179.
²⁶ Augustine, *The City of God*, trans. Rev. Marcus Dods, pp. 1–511 in *St. Augustine's City of God and Christian Doctrine*, vol. 2 of *A Select Library of The Nicene and Post-Nicene Fathers of The Christian Church*, first series, ed. Philip Schaff (Buffalo: The Christian Literature Company, 1887; reprint Grand Rapids: Eerdmans, 1979) 8.14 and 8.16.
²⁷ Ibid. 10.21f.
²⁸ Ibid. 1.24; 3.9; 4.33; 5.1,19,21; 14.27; 18.2.
²⁹ Peter Brown, *Augustine of Hippo* (note 14 above), p. 176.
³⁰ Ibid., pp. 209, 235f.
³¹ Augustine, *The City of God* 19.24–27; 15:4f.
³² Ibid. 20.2.
³³ Ibid. 1.10,30f; 2.20f; 3.10f; 18.2.
³⁴ Ibid. 5.13,15,17f.

[35] Ibid. 1.9; 1.35.

[36] Ibid. 17.13; 18.2; 3.9; 14.27.

[37] See the principles explained in Harvey K. McArthur, *Understanding the Sermon on the Mount* (New York: Harper & Brothers, 1960).

[38] Augustine, *The Preaching of Augustine: "Our Lord's Sermon on the Mount,"* The Preacher's Paperback Library, ed. Jaroslav Pelikan, trans. Francine Cardman (Philadelphia: Fortress Press, 1973) 19.58; 19.59; 19.61 (serm. 19, pp. 66–71).

[39] Ibid. 19.58.

[40] Ibid. 19.56.

[41] Ibid. 20.67.

[42] Ibid. 20.63f.

[43] For the rootedness of sin in our world, see L. John Topel, "Will It Work—Utopia or Eutopia?" in *The Way to Peace: Liberation Through the Bible* (Maryknoll, N.Y.: Orbis Books, 1979), chapter 10.

[44] Augustine, *Reply to Faustus the Manichean*, trans. Rev. R. Stothert, pp. 155–343 in *St. Augustine: The Writings against the Manicheans and against the Donatists*, vol. 4 of *A Select Library of the Nicene and Post-Nicene Fathers of the Christian Church*, first series, ed. Philip Schaff (Buffalo: The Christian Literature Company, 1887; reprint, Grand Rapids: Eerdmans, 1983) 22.74 (p. 301).

[45] Ibid. 22.76.

[46] Ibid. 22.73–78; Augustine, *City of God* 1.26; Morton Kelsey, *Myth, History and Faith: The Remythologizing of Christianity* (New York: Paulist Press, 1974), pp. 22 and 30.

[47] Peter Brown, *Augustine of Hippo* (note 14 above) 421–28. See "Letter 220," pp. 102–111 in Augustine, *Letters* volume 5 (letters 204–270), trans. Sr. Wilfrid Parsons, vol. 13 of *The Fathers of the Church: A New Translation*, ed. Roy Joseph Deferrari et al. (New York: Fathers of the Church, 1956).

[48] The translation for this and the following quotations from *The City of God* is from the edition cited in note 26 above.

[49] Just how difficult this can be is shown by J. Glenn Gray, *The Warriors: Reflections on Men in Battle* (1959; reprint with a new foreword by the author, New York: Harper & Row, Colophon, 1970).

[50] Roland H. Bainton, *Christian Attitudes Toward War and Peace* (see note 7 above), pp. 49f. A major proponent of active nonviolence as a national defense policy today is Gene Sharp. See especially his books *The Politics of Nonviolent Action* (Boston: Porter Sargent,

1973), *National Security Through Civilian-Based Defense* (Omaha, Nebr.: Association for Transarmament Studies [Civilian-Based Defense Association], 1985), *Social Power and Political Freedom* (Boston: Porter Sargent, 1980), and *Making Europe Unconquerable: The Potential of Civilian-Based Deterrence and Defence* (Cambridge, Mass.: Ballinger, 1985). The Civilian-Based Defense Association (formerly Association for Transarmament Studies), 3636 Lafayette, Omaha, Nebraska 68131 publishes a newsletter: "Civilian-Based Defense: News and Opinion." For a more popular treatment of the ideas involved in active nonviolence, civilian-based defense, and transarmament see Ronald J. Sider and Richard K. Taylor, "Is Nonmilitary Defense Possible?" "How Nonmilitary Defense Works," and "Defending the United States by Nonmilitary Means," in *Nuclear Holocaust and Christian Hope* (New York: Paulist Press, 1982), chaps. 13, 14, 15.

[51] Thomas Aquinas, *Summa Theologica*, trans. Fathers of the English Dominican Province (New York: Benziger Brothers, 1947–48) 2a–2ae Q. 40 A. 1 (vol. 2 pp. 1359–60).

[52] Ibid. 2a–2ae Q. 42 A. 2.

[53] Ibid. 2a–2ae Q. 40 A. 1. Note that, for Thomas, just cause is not restricted to repelling aggression. It is modern discussions that center attention on the question "who started it." Thomas is more nuanced. See Frederick H. Russell, *The Just War in the Middle Ages* (note 7 above).

[54] Thomas Aquinas, *Summa Theologica* 2a–2ae Q. 40 A. 1 answer to second objection.

[55] Ibid. 2a–2ae Q. 42 A. 2, body and answer to third objection.

[56] Ibid. 1a–2ae Q. 105 A. 3.

[57] Ibid. 2a–2ae Q. 40 A. 2.

[58] Martin Luther, *Temporal Authority: To What Extent It Should Be Obeyed*, trans. J. J. Schindel, rev. Walther I. Brandt, pp. 75–129 in Walther I. Brandt, ed., *The Christian in Society II*, vol. 45 of *Luther's Works*, ed. Helmut T. Lehmann (Philadelphia: Muhlenberg Press, 1962), p. 103.

[59] Ibid., p. 95.

[60] Martin Luther, *The Sermon on the Mount (Sermons)*, pp. 1–294 in Jaroslav Pelikan, ed., *Luther's Works*, vol. 21, (Saint Louis, Mo.: Concordia, 1956), p. 105 note 43.

[61] Ibid., p. 113.

[62] Ibid., p. 110. See also p. 108.

[63] Ibid., p. 106. Emphasis added.

[64] Ibid., p. 114. Emphasis added.

[65] Ibid., p. 115. Emphasis added.

[66] Ibid., p. 122.

[67] Martin Luther, *Lectures on Romans,* Library of Christian Classics, Ichthus Edition, trans. and ed. Wilhelm Pauck (Philadelphia: Westminster, 1961), p. 362. His diatribe runs from pp. 360–364. Note that he is not so optimistic about secular authorities in his book *Temporal Authority.*

[68] Ibid. 358 note 1.

[69] See E. B. Allo, *Saint Jean l'Apocalypse,* and Isbon T. Beckwith, *The Apocalypse of John* (note 5 above).

[70] Martin Luther, *Whether Soldiers Too Can Be Saved,* trans. Charles M. Jacobs, rev. Robert C. Schultz, pp. 87–137 in Robert C. Schultz, ed., *The Christian in Society III,* vol. 46 of *Luther's Works,* ed. Helmut T. Lehmann (Philadelphia: Fortress, 1967), pp. 95–96.

[71] Ibid., pp. 132–133.

[72] Ibid., pp. 130–131.

[73] Ibid., pp. 125–126.

[74] Frederick H. Russell, *The Just War in the Middle Ages* (note 7 above) comments that modern theories of just war, especially in their concentration on the question of who started the war, are much less developed than medieval just war thought.

[75] John Calvin, *Institutes of the Christian Religion,* in Library of Christian Classics 20 and 21, ed. John T. McNeill, trans. Ford Lewis Battles (Philadelphia: Westminster, 1960), book 4, ch. 20 (vol. 21, pp. 1485–1521).

[76] I hope to publish elsewhere more extensively my ideas on the modern interpretation of these passages in relation to war, peace, violence, and authority, along with further historical background.

[77] The concept of absolutizing the structure is developed especially by G. B. Caird in *Principalities and Powers: A Study in Pauline Theology,* The Chancellor's Lectures for 1954 at Queen's University, Kingston, Ontario (Oxford: at the Clarendon Press, 1956).

[78] For literature on active nonviolent responses effective enough to constitute a nation's main defense or to overcome entrenched tyranny, see note 50 above.